Spirit Song

The Visionary Wisdom of No-Eyes

Mary Summer Rain

A division of Schiffer Publishing, Ltd.
1469 Morstein Road
West Chester, Pennsylvania 19380 USA

Books in the No-Eyes' series by Mary Summer Rain

Spirit Song
Phoenix Rising
Dreamwalker
Phantoms Afoot

Copyright © 1985 by Mary Summer Rain

First Printing, September 1985
Second Printing, December 1986
Third Printing, April 1987
Fourth Printing, November 1987
Fifth Printing, March 1988
Sixth Printing, June 1988
Seventh Printing, September 1988
Eighth Printing, November 1988
Ninth Printing, June 1989

Distributed by Schiffer Publishing, Ltd.
1469 Morstein Road
West Chester, Pennsylania 19380
Please write for a free catalog
This book may be purchased from the publisher.
Please include $2.00 postage.
Try your bookstore first.

Library of Congress Cataloging in Publication Data

Rain, Mary Summer
    Spirit song.

    1. No-Eyes, 1892?-1984. 2. Chippewa Indians—Biography.
3. Shamans—Colorado—Biography. 4. Chippewa Indians—
Religion and mythology. 5. Chippewa Indians—Medicine.
6. Indians of North America—Religion and mythology.
7. Indians of North America—Medicine. 8. Psychical
research—
Colorado—Biography. I. Title.
E99.C6R2   1985   133.8'092'4   8515894
ISBN: 0-89865-405-X (pbk.)

Printed in the United States of America

Contents

This book is lovingly dedicated to the returned teachers and to the seekers who will cherish their wisdom.

Author's Foreword

As the bitterness of the long hard winter began to melt off the mountainsides, a multitude of streams and creeks gushed forth their icy portents of the coming spring. Although the air still wore a chilling glove, gentle signs and scents encouraged the winter-worn hearts of all those who had dared to courageously travel through the steep ravines and along the precarious ledges of the Rocky Mountains in winter. Such foolhardy journeys were never embarked upon by the People-of-the-Land. They were assuredly safe, warm, and content within the comfortable confines of their winter camps. Who then would possess the daring to risk certain death to traverse such a perilous journey?

In the relatively quiet year of 1805, a tall and willowy Shoshoni woman by the name of Sacajawea was confidently threading her way through the hazardous Rocky Mountains in the silent dead of winter. A band of miserably suffering, yet determined men followed in her every footfall. As the frosty fingers of winter withdrew their touch and the sleeping life began to awaken softly around the exhausted travelers, they reached a point in their journey called Grey's Bay. The group rested a while amid tender shoots of willow and they took welcomed solace in the subtle warmth of the gentle breeze drifting over their rough faces off the Columbia River. The river showed definite signs of engorgement from the runoff of the mountain snows; however, it was still a long way from its cresting point.

The men's physical energies were somewhat regained and their spirits were encouraged and once again rejuvenated. Soon all readied the crude boats for the long haul across the comparatively calm Columbia River. The breath of spring had lightened their hearts and they now began to laugh at the comments and humor each man freely bantered about. As they were engulfed in their merriment, they rounded a heavily wooded bend in the river and nearly collided with a band of painted Chinook Indians. Fear gripped them and was evident in the frozen, terrified faces of the white travelers. They instinctively reached for their nearest weapons, keeping them ready and waiting.

1

The Shoshoni woman calmly rose to her feet, brushed back her flowing, glossy hair and raised her delicate hand in the sign of peace. Sacajawea and the Chinook leader conversed casually in the universally understood sign language. The Chinook leader searched hard and long into the white men's eyes. Tension was as thick as a desert dust devil.

Suddenly he gave a peace sign and nodded to Sacajawea. They were free to share the River Spirit and continue their journey. The men drew in deep breaths of relief as once again, because of the brave and beautiful Shoshoni woman, the Lewis and Clark Expedition had not met with fatality, and was allowed to continue its famed journey into the history books.

Sacajawea continued to lead her wearied followers farther west, while hundreds of miles to the east, her Shoshoni band had comfortably settled in for their winter encampment.

The last raving remnants of winter harassed the sturdy dwellings of the large band. The wind took sadistic pleasure in thrashing and howling; however, the People could not be intimidated nor could they be threatened, as each family warmly clustered around their own blazing fires and took contented delight in bravely listening to the Old Ones weave spine-tingling tales of the fearsome evil spirits and the justice meted out by benevolent Manitous.

While the wind whipped its frigid tail about for more attention and repeatedly spewed forth a blinding blizzard from its frozen and flaring nostrils, one lone lodge on the far edge of the camp was tensely silent. The women inside were purposefully going about well-practiced rituals.

Red Willow was barely sixteen and was about to give birth to the first of her seven children. The pungent scent of various herbs and barks filtered through the warm lodge in snaking circlets of smoke. The women, now finished with their individually appointed tasks, waited. They waited.

Suddenly the spirit of winter had a new contender to compete with for attention. It raged and wailed even louder, raising its volume to a deafening pitch, yet the squeal and cry of the tiny new life won in intensity over winter's greatest efforts. Winter conceded, and everyone rejoiced in their own lodges as the birth cries of Walks-in-Woods was heard strong and clear.

As the seasons passed lovingly over the Shoshoni band and Walks-in-Woods grew to be a beautiful woman with many children of her own, she came to be known as She-Who-Sees. Walks-in-Woods would have visions of many things. She became known to all within the band and many would secretly consult her for everything from names

2

to call their children to the best location for hunting. The visitors were not only her woman friends and relatives; the Council Elders also secretly conferred with her. She became known far and wide, and other band members would travel great distances to speak with the woman of vision.

Walks-in-Woods, or She-Who-Sees, would habitually make long and meaningful treks into the silence of the woods. She would converse with the spirits of the soft-eyed deer and listen to the all-knowing wisdom the mountains whispered to her. She-Who-Sees feared for the People's future. She trembled and shook with the lone knowledge gleaned from the spirits of nature. It heavily burdened her. In her kindly heart, She-Who-Sees felt as though a huge stone filled the space in her breast where once a light and carefree heart beat a happy song.

She-Who-Sees witnessed the dreaded fruition of many of her most horrifying visions. Her daughters married white men. The fur traders, trappers, and trailblazers were becoming increasingly more prevalent. As She-Who-Sees became stooped with age and her lovely hair turned from rich ebony to the color of moonlight, she again witnessed another vision come into reality. The old woman now had seen her granddaughters marry white men.

Of all She-Who-Sees' visions of the future, one terrified her the most. She envisioned her bloodline thinning and thinning into total obscurity. At first she solidly passed it off as a great inner fear. "Surely this dreaded thing would never come to be!"

It is not known exactly what made She-Who-Sees take to her blankets, for records, especially Indian records, were not accurately kept in those days. Word of mouth was the rule of the times. However, it can be well assumed that She-Who-Sees didn't want to be witness to any more of her visions.

As she lay so frail and still upon the robe of her new and unfamiliar lodge, She-Who-Sees feebly glanced around at those who were gathering to keep her death vigil. A shaman was called in, although the family rarely used him any more, and didn't believe in his powers.

It was heart-rending to see the old woman as she moved her dull eyes from face to anxious face, as she hardly recognized any of the red man's characteristics in her family. Where were the strong, high cheekbones? Where were the firm chins and hair the color of raven wings? She saw none of the wonderfully homey faces of her People. She looked pitifully into the strange sky-blue eyes of her grand-daughters. She regretfully remembered her first touch of the silky hair of her first grandson, whose hair was the color of corn.

Amid the overwhelming odors of burning herbs and plants, and the incessant rantings of the bedecked medicine man, a single tear escaped from the wrinkled corner of the old woman's eye and coursed down her leathery cheek. She spoke. A quiet sound emitted from the woman and all leaned closer to hear her words, perhaps her very last.

"I have seen many wondrous things and they all have come to be. Some things have not been so wondrous, yet the spirits did not prevent them too from coming to be. I see my own blood running thin around me. It runs white as winter snows. I see this white blood turning its white back on the People's ways. My heart is on the ground."

The old woman's eyelids softly closed and she dropped her hand to her bony side. She lay still, very still. Those around her looked silently at one another and knew the old one had died. The shaman quieted his gourd and peered at the frail form upon the modern fur-covered bed. She-Who-Sees' relatives knew her visions had indeed come to be. They were not sorry, though, for they knew that this path of the People was inevitable in order for them to survive. They enjoyed the new and convenient ways of the white man and they regarded her as the last of her kind, one who would not, could not change.

Suddenly they were all startled. The old woman moved. She was not finished with her words yet. Again they leaned down closer, putting their ears to her dry lips. The woman's voice came out in a barely audible cracked whisper.

"You, in time, will even deny your birth. Yet, I see one in the future who will still be a part of me and she will shame you all, as she will be as refreshing as a summer rain on the plains. She will not forget the ways of the spirit." The old woman closed her eyes. Now she was free.

Walks-in-Woods, or She-Who-Sees, died at the age of 102. Many years passed and those years brought immense changes for the People-of-the-Land. The old woman's visions and words truly came into being. Those of her bloodline did indeed eventually deny their heritage. It wasn't profitable nor was it socially beneficial for them to do otherwise, or so they thought. They all sought the good life, and that just wasn't possible for an Indian. As the old woman became farther and farther removed from her ensuing generations, it became unthinkable for the People to even remotely consider admitting that they were of Indian descent. Sadly enough, they had successfully convinced even themselves.

I heard this pitiful story several years ago. How I came by it is not important; however, it sporadically interrupted my daily thoughts and continued to weave hauntingly in and out of my dreams. The old woman's coal-black eyes would seem to beckon to me; they would virtually pierce deep into my very soul. I could no longer evade the soft whisperings and hinted-at insinuations that were painfully pulling at my heart.

As time passed slowly over the last few years, I began to take a deeper interest in native American history. I found myself purchasing all manner of Indian items and filling my home with pottery and weavings. My husband thought it was all very interesting and appealing, my three young daughters thought it was unusual yet exciting, and I thought it felt like coming home.

I found it increasingly futile to continue trying to ignore this strange tale. It nagged at me incessantly. It would seem that I could have no inner peace until I delved more deeply into the story. I barely knew where to begin.

I went back to the person I had heard the story from, but all I got for my effort was a dead end. I couldn't find accurate records, as they were obscure or nonexistent. After coming up short time after time, I was ready to give up the search. Perhaps the story was just one of those beautiful Indian legends that are embellished upon as they are passed from mouth to eager mouth.

Yet, one last try certainly couldn't hurt. Again I called the party who had relayed the old woman's story to me. I felt somewhat embarrassed at approaching the story again, yet I swallowed my pride while I prodded for more information. My bruised pride was richly rewarded. The truth of the story was revealed only under strict conditions on my part. I listened intently as the hair on my neck prickled and my heart raced to the feverish pace of war drums. I gratefully thanked the person on the other end of the line and softly hung up the receiver. I sat for what must have been a very long while. So many visions and thoughts had to be sorted out, yet one thing was clear: I couldn't forget the old woman nor her wise ways. I wouldn't forget She-Who-Sees, for she was my ancestral grandmother and I am Summer Rain. I won't forget you, old grandmother. You have seen to that. I love you.

A Woman Called Bright Eyes

*May your moccasins cross the
threshold of Truth,
And may your trail lead into the
beauty beyond.*

It was autumn. And although the lateness of the season would normally be giving witness to the coming harshness of a cruel, hard winter, the small Chippewayan encampment was enjoying the Earth Mother's golden gift of a glorious extended Indian summer. It was indeed a rarity for this northern Minnesota region to experience such balmy weather so late in the season. Yet, many new changes were being felt by the People now.

Changes were foretold by the voices on the wind. Changes were prophesied by the wizened old shamans. Changes were about everywhere; some already finding their ugly twisted way into the present, while others were slowly coursing their sure-footed way into the village.

The tiny village was nestled comfortably between the Place-of-Still-Waters and the Red Mountains. The village elders held many regular councils to discuss the future of the small band. The white soldiers were everywhere, and freedom for the People had to be cherished moment by precious moment. Even though they had been settled a mere three weeks, it would appear by the wind's warnings that very soon they would once again be on the move—but to where? Lately this was a grave problem..

While the men talked and argued late into the night, Pretty Weasel was deep in the throes of her first and only labor. She was

7

having trouble. She had dutifully followed the medicine woman's explicit instructions, yet something was very wrong. She knew it. Her tired attendants knew it. And Yellow Bird Woman, the medicine woman, knew it. Finally, after an herb was given to Pretty Weasel as a last resort, a tiny baby girl entered the world of the Chippewas. Pretty Weasel was now exhausted, yet exhilarated to have it over.

Yellow Bird Woman carefully examined the new child. She sadly looked from the sober face of one attendant to the next and merely shook her head. She applied a common mixture of herbs and mud to the infant's eyes, spat upon the dark mass and wiped it away. She peered into the tiny eyes. Again she shook her head.

"Where's my baby?" asked Pretty Weasel.

The medicine woman cradled the small form in its mother's waiting arms. Immediately it began to eagerly suckle.

"The little one is perfect in every way except one," Yellow Bird Woman said softly. "She will never see from her eyes, but her mind will see things we cannot."

Pretty Weasel then knew she had given birth to a special child. A child who would have a purpose to her life. This was a great thing. Usually one never knew their purpose until they experienced a vision, yet this tiny being, only minutes old, already knew. Pretty Weasel was honored and proud with a big heart.

The child quietly nursed as Yellow Bird Woman finished her work on the new mother. "Pretty Weasel, this will be your only child. You cannot have more," she said.

Pretty Weasel smiled down upon the wee hungry child. "I accept this. I have all I need. I call her Bright Eyes, for she will see wondrous things."

The year was 1892.

As it happened, the small village was able to remain by the Place-of-Still-Waters near the Red Mountains. And the many bitter winters came and went.

The little blind baby grew to girlhood with ease and to early maturity with grace. She had few friends to play with, as the girl called Bright Eyes was different. She knew many personal things about the other young girls and, of course, they didn't like that.

Pretty Weasel cared for her daughter alone. She never married, nor did she ever speak to Bright Eyes about her father. That fact did not seem to bother the young girl. Her days were full of learning and sensing so many things. She lived her life with her mother and they shared many beautiful times together.

Together they enjoyed fishing and hunting. The senses of Bright Eyes were so keen she often heard the animals before her mother did.

Pretty Weasel taught her daughter all she needed to know about living by herself. She told Bright Eyes all the wonderful legends and stories of their glorious past. Together they sat by their warm fireside and laughed and shared with one another. Together they were totally content and self-sufficient.

The village remained unchanged for fourteen years before the inevitable encroachment of the white society caught up with them. They were remote but not remote enough. The white man's government sent representative agents into the secluded village. The Indian children were now required to attend the white man's schools. The children needed to learn the white man's tongue and ways of living. The forestalled changes came at last.

Pretty Weasel was frightened by the new changes she saw occurring in her village. How could she send her blind child to a white man's school? What did they know that Bright Eyes already didn't? Pretty Weasel talked it over with her daughter and together, under the complete cover of a new moon, the two left the village they had called their home for fourteen years.

Higher and higher into the mountains they climbed. When they were deep into the forest they stopped at a place where they thought it would be safe. Then, just to be absolutely certain, they went in further and deeper.

For days and days they labored. They collected fallen logs for a crude house structure and they fashioned criss-crossed branches covered with thick brush for a roof. They worked dried grasses in with mud and solidly chinked in the spaces of the walls. Several skins sewn together served as a door covering. They were ingenious and industrious—they had to be, necessity made them that way. And when all was finished, the two weary women were pleased with their new home. Most of all, they were proud of their ability to continue their freedom.

Again they worked together to sustain their lives. Again they were able to laugh and enjoy their simple way of living. The sun was warm on their faces and Father Sky smiled lovingly down on them. What more could they want? They were even blessed with an occasional visitor.

Two Trees was the village shaman. He was aging now and his apprentice was prepared to become the chief shaman. The elder medicine man found himself away from the village more and more these days, especially now since the white man's ways were replacing so many of the long-ago ways of the Indians' glorious time-honored traditions. It was a useless fight. He found no inner energy left to battle these new people. Yes, he knew their strange tongue, but that was the most he would allow the two cultures to mix. Never could they mix.

Two Trees made a regular habit of visiting Pretty Weasel and her gifted daughter, Bright Eyes. He would always bring fresh rabbit and fish for the two women. At times he would spend as long as a week with them. They would talk long into the night about their beautiful ways that would now appear to be vanished forevermore. Two Trees made improvements on the women's house and strengthened their roof. It wasn't long before he was up in the mountains more than he was in the village. He could see his usefulness waning and finally went up into the mountains never to return to the village again.

Perhaps the villagers thought the old shaman walked into the forest to die, as that was often the custom. However, Two Trees was not yet prepared to die. He had more work to do. His time had not yet come. Two Trees built himself a home about a half-mile from Pretty Weasel and her daughter. The two neighbors took great comfort knowing the other was there, knowing the other remained free.

One summer morning when Bright Eyes was sixteen, she accompanied her mother to a nearby pond where the cattails were growing profusely. The two commented on the particularly beautiful day and their hearts were filled with a fullness that only comes from joy and total contentment.

A sudden frown wrinkled the smooth brow of the youthful Bright Eyes.

Pretty Weasel noticed the change. "And what enemy disturbs our wonderful day?"

"I was wondering how many more moons life will be like this. I was thinking of changes, mother."

Pretty Weasel smoothed her daughter's glossy hair. "Must you let your mind bring an enemy into our day? Each day is new and we cannot keep the changes away forever. We can only be thankful for each day we are free to live as we like. The tomorrows will take care of themselves. Come, we are here and the tubers are ripe for digging."

Bright Eyes was soothed by her mother's wisdom. She began digging in the muddy shoulder of the pond. Suddenly the young woman stopped digging and lifted her face to the sun.

Pretty Weasel had become accustomed to her daughter's sightless visions. She also stopped her digging. She waited respectfully until the young woman was ready to reveal what she had seen.

Bright Eyes looked to the sky. Her mind saw a large cloud forming and soon she was totally entranced by it. She began her familiar travel. Her small feet left the cool dampness of the ground. She floated effortlessly up to the cloud. She entered. Many villages were assembled inside, all peacefully living together. Everyone was dressed alike. Everyone wore the Ghost Dance shirts. She mingled among the people until a great chief joined her and walked with her to his tepee. Inside, the skin walls were decorated with complex and strange symbols, signs she had never before seen. They sat.

He spoke softly. "It is time for Bright Eyes to be about her business. You will take a long journey to the mountains far away in the west. You will bring the wisdom out of the hearts of those who find you. You will keep alive our ways. But first you must learn many of the old ways. Two Trees, your father, will teach you all you need to know. You are blind but see all you need to see. Go now, you have much to do."

Bright Eyes was again on the wet grass by the pond. She turned slowly to face her mother. "My father has much to teach me, mother, I have much to learn before I leave here."

Pretty Weasel held her daughter close. She was glad the young woman finally knew who her father was. It was a terrible offense for the shaman to have loved a women, hence the need for secrecy. Now that the vision had lifted the heavy burden from her shoulders, nothing was held back between them. The two finished their gathering and returned home.

Pretty Weasel listened intently as her daughter relayed the unusual vision. They spent a long while discussing it. They planned late into the evening. Many changes were now in the wind.

Bright Eyes tossed and turned the whole of that night. Her dreams were filled with strange people. She saw herself living alone until she was very old. Great visionaries of all the tribes weaved in and out to talk with her. She saw herself teaching people the old ways. She held protective control over the spirits of darkness. She easily communicated with the spirits of light and the entities of power. Bright Eyes was restless to be about her business.

Pretty Weasel also fitfully tossed and turned on her bed. She knew her daughter was now truly a woman. She knew she wouldn't be seeing much more of her. She was proud to be the mother of such a one as Bright Eyes. Yet, she had a heart heavy with sadness. Her daughter had a great burden. The Great Spirit must watch over her.

Shortly before the long orange arms of dawn touched the two women's rooftop, Pretty Weasel and Bright Eyes were caressed by the completeness of sleep and it swept them into its loving peacefulness.

It wasn't meant for Bright Eyes to leave so soon. She remained living with Pretty Weasel for many more glorious years. However, all her days were spent with her father, the shaman, Two Trees. She learned of the healing properties of the Earth Mother's bountiful plants. She labored long and hard to free her spirit and journey to places never before dreamed of. She attuned her keen senses, switched mental vibratory gears, and found herself in planes and dimensions of different existing realities. She discovered complex truths regarding the fine essence of time—only the physical body experiences the present, yet the spirit experiences past and future. She learned to find the narrow veil opening which allowed her spirit to converse with those who were no longer in the physical boundary. She used various colors and precise tones to heal. Emotions were studied. Nature was studied. She studied herself. After ten years of intensive learning, Two Trees had no more to teach her. His job was done. Hers was just beginning.

Pretty Weasel finished her preparations for Bright Eyes' long journey. The young woman was now twenty-six and was going to accompany several of the adventurous villagers who were traveling to the West. Many of the People were moving about freely now and they weren't as desirous to remain in one place as they once were. The world was open to them. And they took advantage of it whenever they could. Bright Eyes left with friends and journeyed on a long train ride that took many days.

Pretty Weasel and Two Trees moved into one house. The old shaman kept a close watch on his daughter's whereabouts and her activities. The couple grew older together and Two Trees would often speak to Pretty Weasel out of the blue. "Bright Eyes is in a nice cabin today. She is learning new plants." Another time he would suddenly announce, "Bright Eyes met someone good. She is a good teacher." He kept very close tabs on her progress. He was proud of her accomplishments. Now he was prepared to die in peace.

The Woodland Crossroad

*May your winding path be crossed
by a wise one,
And may your Spirits perceive
recognition.*

One bright spring morning in the Rocky Mountains of Colorado, when the tiny aspen buds still looked like fuzzy gray pussywillows, an old woman was enjoying her regular meditative walk through her woods when she sensed a new presence. She froze and searched with her mind. She watched silently, unnoticed by the presence.

A young woman with long dark hair was quietly sitting on a log and crying. The woman evidently thought she was alone. After all, it was a rarely traveled section of the forest—practically virgin in the sense of human use. The woman on the log then realized she wasn't alone. She saw the old woman standing in the shadows. She was startled.

The old woman spoke first. "You lost?"

"No," came the unsure reply.

"You look for someone lost?"

"No."

"You hungry?"

"No."

"That all you can say?"

"No. I mean I came here to be alone. I didn't know many others came here. Do you come here often?"

The old woman nodded. "I don't just come here. I live here. This my home."

The young woman expressed her surprise to find out the old Indian lived in such a secluded section of the wilderness. Her mood changed. "How many people live up here?"

"One. Me," came the short reply.

"You? All alone?"

"What so 'bout that?" she defended.

Now the younger woman realized the old Indian was also blind. "You're blind!"

"Not like *you!* You just now see that I blind?" she snapped.

"I'm sorry. That was really rude of me. If this is your property I'll leave. You obviously want to be alone too." She turned and began walking away.

The old one let the younger one walk off. She let her spirit search for the needed information. Then she shouted, "SUMMER RAIN!"

I whipped around in shocked amazement. The old woman somehow knew my name. The name nobody called me. The name my great-grandmother used only once in my life. My mouth hung open in disbelief.

The old one motioned for me to come closer. She had a knowing grin on her face. "You come. We go my cabin. We talk, huh?"

I was still mentally numbed. I followed the woman through the woods that she obviously knew like the back of her wrinkled hand. My mind began to thaw by degrees. And in the silence that followed I wondered how this stranger knew my other name.

"I tell that at cabin," she replied matter-of-factly. She had this odd grin creeping up the grooved corners of her mouth which revealed narrow pink gums.

I couldn't help grinning back at the humorous sight of her.

"Some stuff funny?"

"Why no. Actually, yes. This whole thing is so incredible!" I admitted.

"Humph!" was all she mumbled.

We walked into a clearing and crossed an old weed-covered road. At the crest of a small rise was a crude log cabin with a covered porch.

"We here," she stated as she led me up the hill and over her time-worn steps.

Once inside she motioned for me to sit on her Salvation Army couch while she continued into her small kitchen.

I wondered at the wisdom of my decision to follow the old

woman. Maybe she was nuts. Maybe I was to be her next victim. You hear and read about so many hideous things these days. I was becoming extremely over-anxious to leave.

"I *not* nuts! Nuts out *there!*" she shouted, pointing a knobby finger out the window. "Summer read 'bout nuts out there. You see. We talk. First I make good tea."

The old biddy had shouted at me. That scared me. But what really scared me more was when I realized she was reading my mind. My God, she could hear my thoughts!

"Yup," came the affirmative admission.

My mind raced faster than the cars at the Indianapolis 500. Who or what was I dealing with here? Who *was* this lonely old blind woman? Who indeed?

"I get to that. I get to *all* that. First we have tea." She returned to the living area, gave me my drink, and sat herself down in a rickety rocker that needed major repairs. It broke our uncomfortable silence with its rhythmic creak and thud. She was blind, yet looked directly through me. "I know who you are. Do you know who you are?"

"Of course I know who I am," I defended.

"Blah! You only *think* you know who you are. Many peoples here now. They not know who they are either. I know." She sipped her drink and rocked.

I looked into her eyes and didn't see insanity. I didn't recognize any semblance of it at all. Yet there was something there I did see that I didn't understand. Something I'd never seen behind anyone else's eyes—not ever.

"Summer see herself," she stated simply.

"Who *are* you?" I asked softly.

"You never answered *me.*"

"Yes I did. I said I did know who I was."

"That no answer. You know that no answer. You still never say who you are," she insisted.

"I'm Summer Rain. Who are you?"

"I Bright Eyes, Chippewa from Minnesota. Where *you* from?"

"Michigan originally, now I live in Woodland Park."

"Where?"

"Woodland Park."

"That not what I mean. *Where* you from?"

I was becoming extremely frustrated with this entire nonsensical conversation that couldn't get off its insane merry-go-round. I sighed.

"Okay, we talk some other thing. You not ready to admit where you from yet—maybe you not even know yet. We get to that later.

Why you in woods today?"

"I wanted to be alone," I hinted.

"Never alone. Peoples never alone. Somebody always there," she said softly as she crossed the small room and sat beside me. She put a wrinkled hand on my lap. "Summer, our paths cross today for good reason. You not first person come here. I meet others in my woods who want to be alone. We make good friends. I teach many things. They remember who they are, where they come from, why they here. We spend many days together, many nights even. We go many places up here." She pointed to her forehead. "Summer sent here too. We talk. You learn too."

I wasn't stupid. I wasn't ignorant of the infinite chances on fate's wheel. My husband, Bill, and I had done years and years of reading, searching, studying. We had some paranormal functioning and I knew these things happened. I knew there were many people with abilities that couldn't be simply explained. Consequently, the gravity of what the old woman was saying was slowly sinking through my thick head. Simply stated, she was a spiritual teacher and I was destined to meet her. I literally began to tremble with an uncontrollable excitement. I had waited so long to share certain things with someone who knew what I was talking about, with someone who understood. It's so lonely living among the unaware of the world. I shook. And I was embarrassed.

"That good sign," she said as her small brown hand quivered along with my shaking knee. "That show you know I say truth. That say you believe. That say it all, Summer." She grinned.

All I could do was smile.

She grinned wider and patted my lap.

A certain warmth flooded through to the very core of my being. The trembling continued but I didn't care. It was my natural physical response to an encounter with a person who possessed a like spirit. It was my foolproof personal barometer of spirit recognition. It was embarrassing, yet beautiful at the same time. I realized the old lady was respectfully waiting until I had sorted out the maze of thoughts that were twisting through my mind. Perhaps she was joining me through that maze. I suspect that she was. At any rate, I was thrilled to death to have met her (destined or otherwise). I knew this was *it* for me. Finally I had solid access to understanding the finer aspects of so many complex theories and concepts. Finally I would be on my way to a perfect understanding of them and of myself. Perhaps this old teacher could even pinpoint my purpose—something that had been a nebulous nagging in the forefront of my mind for years.

"Summer find that herself. I no tell that. I *know* that but I no tell.

That come from inside, here." She again pointed to her forehead.

I smiled knowingly. Of course I knew nobody on earth can tell another what their purpose is. I believed the old one knew what mine was. I also believed she was going to be vitally instrumental in bringing me to a point where I would find it deep within myself. I knew in my heart that this wrinkled being and I were going to be spending a great deal of time together, we would become good friends.

She squeezed my knee. "We be good friends, maybe even better. You see. Now, why you cry in woods?"

I had the distinct feeling that Bright Eyes already knew the answers to any question she asked. "I think you know why, Bright Eyes."

"Humph! That no reason not to talk. Maybe I do. Maybe I know, what so! How we gonna talk if I talk to myself? I gonna ask Summer questions and I gonna answer too? When Summer gonna talk, huh?"

Her way of speaking was so comical. She would say "what so" instead of "so what." I understood her meaning and played along with the wise one. I answered her questions, questions that she already knew the answers to. Later on, when I was alone to think about our day together, I realized that her uncanny ability wouldn't allow any room for little white lies.

"I was crying because I'm frustrated with life."

"That only top of problem. Dig down more."

"Everything I do is blocked somehow. I can't seem to break through the barrier. I feel like I'm always batting my head against a wall. I get so far and I think I'm going to win when suddenly a giant barrier goes up and I'm stopped cold in my tracks again. It's so devastating. This has been going on for seven years. I was crying because I feel so helpless against them. They always win."

The old woman took my cup and led me to her porch. We sat in the sun that was warming the steps. "They not always win, Summer. They not always gonna win with you. They done winning with you. It *your* turn now."

I would dearly love to believe that. The sun felt good and soothing on my tired body. I let it envelop me. I sighed.

"Summer, I know who you are. You know too. You feel it here." She pounded my chest. "Others know who you are. They on wrong side. They not want peoples like you to win. They have powerful medicine. Summer, *your* medicine more powerful. You win. You see, soon."

"If only that was true."

"It so! I know. Many peoples like you here now. They not come to sit and lose. They come to win! Summer, I tell you something big going on. Something right here in mountains. It not here yet. Voices in wind tell Bright Eyes great things. Bright Eyes move into coming days. I see it. Peoples all over like you getting ready for great thing. You feel it. I know you feel it."

"All I feel is such a tremendous urgency to get going. I feel a terrific pressure to move on, to get about my business. I'm so frightened when I think of the future. Bright Eyes, I get so scared. I need to win *now!* Time is too short."

"How you know time too short? Who tell Summer that, huh?"

"Isn't that sort of question irrelevant? I think you know what I mean. The signs are all about us, Bright Eyes. Things are going down just the way it's been foretold. Every day brings us closer. The closer we get, the more pressure I feel. *Nobody* has to tell me these things. They're right out in front for all to see. And I'm about done pushing myself."

"Summer give up? What Summer do?"

"I don't know, I really don't. I've thought of so many ways of leaving I can't count them all. Yet, I'm held back when I think of my kids and Bill. Sometimes we've even considered going together. Bright Eyes, the pressure of this is so great and the battles with the others have worn us down time and time again. Bill had the idea of leaving in our sleep to let others come to continue in our place. But then, when I think of all the battles we've fought, what would it be for if we then let another take our place to finish the purpose? *We* should be the ones to finish what we came to do. I don't believe our spirits would rest knowing we gave up, gave over our purpose to others. So, here we stay to see it through, yet the pressures are so great and the urgency of time weighs so heavily on us."

"Do you think you alone in this?"

"No. We know the others here are feeling the same things. But that knowledge doesn't make it any more comforting, you know. Just thinking that others are having the same frustrating battles makes it worse. Why can't we all manage to get into position when things are so close? Why does it have to go down to the wire every time? I just don't understand it."

"All in the Great Spirit's time, Summer, all in His time."

"But we've so much to do . . . ."

"That where I come in. You learn fast from me." She bent close to my face and whispered. "We get like snake in grass. We slip by those others. They not even know you cross battleline. You win after all. I know many ways to fool those others. You see, Summer, you see."

I was given a ray of hope to grasp onto. And I did, with all my remaining strength.

She wasn't finished. "All of you peoples will be in position when time counts. I know other peoples here. They be with you, help you. A great brotherhood of mountains will be center for many peoples seeking truths. Summer be big part."

"When? Where? Bright Eyes, I don't doubt, but there are certain things needed for this. . . ."

"Summer *do* doubt!" she interrupted angrily. "Summer *fail* with that kind of dumb mind! Summer know so much, Summer not *think!* No can give up no matter how things look now! I see! I know what coming! What so about the others. I get you through."

I too knew what was coming and it scared the pants off me. So little time to do so much.

"That not way to think. Summer and good man *will* win! I see many day, many night work for Summer. We get it done together. Together we beat time."

I listened. I hoped. I think I even believed. I desperately wanted to.

"Summer know I right, huh Summer?"

"I believe you are capable of helping us. I believe you know things that can't be found in any books. I believe you can help."

"I do more than help. I be good friend, Summer. I open doors and slip you through, some doors I slip you under. Brotherhood of mountains no good without Summer. We bring it out of future into *now.*"

I had the sudden inclination to hug the old wrinkled one. She has such incredible positive and loving vibrations coming from her. She would be my lifeline, my lone spiritual lifesaver on the turbulent sea of the psychic warzone that we had been trying to tread for so long. I grabbed it and held on for dear life. Not just for *my* life, but for the life of my purpose, for the life of those who would remain to endure the coming horrors—the final autumn of man.

I hugged the small mass of old skin and creaky bones. I cried as she wrapped her thin arms about me and patted my head. It was as if I had found the reincarnation of my ancestral grandmother, She-Who-Sees. It was as if time had pulled together the years separating her day and mine. We were one in purpose. We were one in mind. We were one in spirit.

And so went the meeting of two people: one ageless with the timeless knowledge, one fledgling, only beginning.

I drove home that spring evening with a new fire in my spirit. A fire as bright as the brilliant orange fire that blazed in the evening western sky.

Voices of Truth

*May your sight be as straight
as an arrow,
And may all your arrows aim at Truth.*

Driving home that evening after my first meeting with No-Eyes (the name she asked me to use instead of her real name) gave me some needed space to do a lot of heavy thinking. How ironic it was. I had gone into the woods that morning feeling a total isolation from the world. I was in a deep depression as I had once again felt my back was up against that cold hard wall. Yet now, when I left the woods I was exhilarated, excited, and full of a marvelous renewed hope. It was as if while leaning against that wall it had miraculously come equipped with a hidden door. And, falling through, I discovered my opening to the future. I was riding on cloud nine all the way home.

When I got there I sat Bill down and calmly brought him through my amazing day. I told him how I initially thought the old woman was insane. How I even mentally referred to her as an old biddy. I spoke of her broken English and how humorous her transposed phrases were. Best of all, I relayed the beautiful things she said to me.

Immediately Bill recognized the signs. He too was anxious about this wise woman who appeared to be destined to teach us more and to assist us in our purpose. God worked in strange ways and in His own time—but He worked all the same.

We made plans for me to visit the old one regularly. I would talk with her and learn all I could from her. Then I would recount the lessons and share them with Bill. In this manner we would both equally reap the woman's knowledge.

I would like to take a moment here to say that I have been blessed with the perfect lifemate. Bill and I were high school sweethearts and were married at nineteen. We've had a financially difficult life; however, our kindred spirits have taken great solace in each other during all the tremendously hard times. We have always shared every little thought. Never have we held back secrets from one another—ever. I believe we are unique. Later on, No-Eyes told me that when we were yet in the spirit plane before this present incarnation, Bill readily volunteered for a purpose here and I wanted to be with him again. She also told me that we have been together as lifemates in many previous lifetimes. When I was able to view the Book of Records for myself, I saw this to be true. No wonder we fit together so well.

We excitedly made plans for me to visit No-Eyes the following day. We didn't see any sense in wasting time; we felt enough time had been wasted already—too much time. Sleep was long in coming that night. We both tossed and turned.

It proved to be another beautiful spring morning. This is quite a feat, for in the Colorado mountains spring is usually wet with heavy snow. The glorious sun was shining brightly when I took off for the long drive into the National Forest. I was filled with weighted anticipation. The world once again looked as clean and innocent as a newborn babe. Indeed, signs of rebirth were in evidence everywhere I looked. The aspens were sprouting their fuzzy buds. Plump birds hopped along the roadside. Sprouts of green grasses glistened with their shower of dew. The willows set up light green spikes of new growth. And the new hope fluttered within my heart like a swarm of playful butterflies. It was good. It was so good again.

I was able to find the weed-choked road that led near the woman's hill. I had to park some distance away, as boulders had rolled in its pathway. I got out and let the crisp mountain morning air refresh my senses. Birds were everywhere. Squirrels chased each other up and down the pines in a mischievous game of tag. Activity thrived. I thrived. The mountains made me thrive. They gave me life.

I tore myself away from the beauty of the woods and ascended the small hill to the cabin. I crossed the porch and gently knocked.

No answer.

I knocked again, only louder. Perhaps she was a little hard of hearing.

No answer.

I peeked through the windows. The curtains were pulled, however the tattered material was a type of open weave. It was dark inside, yet I could make everything out. I didn't see No-Eyes anywhere. I knocked again, harder still.

"You wanna break that door?" The old one came up out of the woods behind me.

I turned, rather surprised. "Hi. I was just beginning to think you weren't home."

"Where I go? Out for drive somewheres? Anyways, you late!"

I looked disbelieving at her. "Late! I didn't even tell you I was coming up here this morning. How can I be late?"

"I know you come today. I think you be here much earlier. Summer not anxious to begin?"

"I am anxious to begin. When should've I gotten here?"

"Before sun here, that when. Summer need to learn how to greet new day. No can do now, sun already been greeted." She shrugged her narrow shoulders and walked past me into the cabin. She came back into the doorway. "You gonna stand out there all day?"

She sure had a rude-sounding way of speaking. I attributed it to her lack of understanding of the English usage. I quickly joined her in the cabin.

"I no need speak better. I know what I say. Summer have much to learn. No time for small talk."

I grinned. "Thought you said we had plenty of time."

She frowned. "You think you smart! You not! You just have smart mouth, that all."

I was definitely in trouble. I was merely trying to break the ice by playing with her. She had quickly put me in my place. Students don't play—they learn. "I'm sorry. I didn't mean it the way it must've sounded."

"I know how meant. I not stupid like some peoples I know." She looked through me and grinned. We had made our peace.

So she did understand the language after all. She was a clever one, she was. However, I must watch my verbal bantering with her. This was a habit with me and I realized that this wise woman was all business, except when *she* initiated the humor.

"Come sit."

I sat on the old couch while she pulled over her rocker. We were now directly facing one another. She was doing something in her mind. Maybe sizing me up. Perhaps gauging my ability to learn. Whatever she was doing didn't take long. She looked into my eyes. It was uncanny. If I didn't know better I would've thought she was physically seeing me. She rested back in the rocker but it remained still.

"How you know I what I say?" she began.

"I feel it. Yesterday you even said my shaking was a good sign. I know it is a signal of recognition for me. I do know you're what you say you are."

"What that?"

I thought a minute. "Well, I only just met you, but by the way our conversation went yesterday, I know you're aware of certain things few people are. You knew my thoughts. You see without sight. You're here as a spiritual teacher."

"Humph!"

Whatever that meant I didn't know. I was to hear many of them in the months to come.

"You pretty smart."

"No, just feelings is all," I softly admitted.

"Summer always believes feelings?"

"Yes."

"Why?"

"Because my feelings are truer than my physical senses. My feelings guide my conscious thought."

"Why?"

I had the distinct impression this verbal circle dance was leading somewhere besides around and around. And I wasn't able to jump off to discover where—yet.

"How Summer know feelings truer? Summer not listen to mind?"

"Only when the mind agrees with the feelings."

"Humph!" She rocked a minute and allowed the creak and thump meter to break our silence. "You gonna do fine."

I smiled. "I hope so."

"*Hope!* You not hope! Summer say *yes!*"

"Yes, I'll do fine."

"That better." Again the lopsided sound stopped. Her tone was softer. "Summer, what we gonna do here be serious stuff. If you no listen good, you get hurt. I not like repeating stuff. It good you trust truth in feelings. My words no good if Summer no believe. Summer have to feel truth in all stuff here." She pounded her chest. "If Summer no believe, it no good. No-Eyes never say lies. All stuff I speak is truth. Summer need to believe all stuff here."

"I see."

"That not good enough. Summer have to believe!"

"I believe it's important I have to believe. What if you say something I don't believe?"

"What so! Then I prove. But Summer believe all stuff anyway. Summer know truth when she hear it. I no speak lies anyway."

"Alright."

"So! What truth? You tell me." She began rocking, waiting.

I attempted an honest answer. "Truth is something you feel is right. You feel it in your spirit. It's a kind of inner knowing."

"That okay for you. How 'bout other peoples who no *feel* truth? How they gonna know truth when they hear it?"

"I suppose those people have to use their physical minds. They have to weigh what they've heard or read against what they already know, their experiences and their common logic."

"What so if they no have this experience or good logic? How they gonna know truth then, huh Summer?"

"I suppose they would then trust someone of authority on the subject in question."

"What if that someone lie?"

Silence.

"Well, Summer?"

Silence. Thinking.

Creak-thud. Creak-thud.

She had me solidly stumped. How *do* some people recognize truth?

"I ask Summer that one. Guess Summer not know."

"Guess not."

"Peoples always looking, reading, hearing for truth. They read and read. What so if books lie? They listen and listen. What so if talker lie? They look and look. What so if end lie? They lost. They never find truth. It not in books. It not in special teacher. It not in one religion. Truth stuff *have* to come from inside all persons. Every persons have truths inside when they come here. Peoples must learn that. You say peoples need logic, experiences to know truth. I say blah! Great Spirit plant truth in all peoples' spirit when they born. Not born here, born in beginning. All peoples have great ability to know truth. They look under rugs. They look behind trees. They look in all wrong places for truth. It inside all along!"

"But people don't know that, No-Eyes."

"They know. They just lazy. Summer not lazy, huh?"

"No."

"Summer go see truth."

"Where?"

"Go see truth. Out there!" She pointed a long finger and made a sweeping motion with her arm.

I got up.

"*Sit down!* Where Summer think she going?"

"You said outside," I defended nervously.

"You no hear good! I no say outside! I say out there."

I was embarrassed. I felt like a real dumb student. Already I was being chastised for not listening properly, and justly so I might add.

She ignored the reprimand and continued as if nothing had transpired. "Now, we sit back and relax body. We breathe up long, then down long. That right. Now, think all body stuff made of air. No heavy nothing. That good."

We waited at this point. I sensed her in my mind, following my every mental maneuver. She was fantastic.

"Now, think body lighter than air."

I imagined my entire being composed of helium. All I thought was helium, helium. And together we were outside of the small cabin. No-Eyes was next to me smiling. She now had brilliant, beautiful eyes that sparkled with clear sight. She led me up past the treetops, up through wispy clouds, up past the light of the sun and into the vastness of space.

I had done this on my own before, but never so fast and certainly never with such simple ease. The old one appeared to be a psychic catalyst of sorts. Just her simple presence made my efforts so simple.

She pointed to an enormous object in space. We drifted over to it and entered effortlessly through its outer shell. Inside, many foreign-looking beings were busily going about appointed tasks. We hovered about here and there. Large screens depicted different areas of the Earth. It appeared to me that these beings were observing; no, more like guarding the secret doings of the various governments. She motioned for us to leave. Again we were in the vast expanse of space. We began to descend. Back down past the sun, through the clouds and through her cabin roof. I opened my eyes.

No-Eyes was watching me. She was cleverly observing my reactions.

"Where did we go?" I asked.

"We? *We* no go anywhere."

"Are you saying that I just fell asleep and dreamed that?"

"Nope."

"Didn't we go out there?"

"What *you* say?"

"I say you and I went out there!" I pointed to the ceiling.

"Nope," came the disappointing reply.

"What do you mean, nope?"

"What truth, Summer? What really happen?"

"I felt myself leaving. That's truth. I saw you next to me. That's truth. You and I wen . . ."

"Nope."

"You *were* next to me!"

"You *feel* that?"

I thought a minute. A trick? No, I *saw* her next to me but I never *felt* her there. My God, was she even with me? Was I alone?

"Yep."

My stupid mouth hung open.

"Thought Summer only believe what felt?"

"But how did you do that? You made me believe something that wasn't even there."

"I no make Summer believe no thing. Summer do that all by herself. Think!"

She was right, of course. She never came right out and said she was there with me—never even said she was going! What a sneaky lady.

"You figure stuff out yet?"

I nodded sheepishly.

"Summer caught off guard. Never take one thing for granted in lessons or in life. *Never* assume! *Never* believe *no* stuff until Summer *feel* it! This most greatest lesson. We gonna do many things. We gonna go many places. Some places scare Summer. Summer *have* to know what she feels to know what true—what *not* there. This always be first lesson. It most important. We gonna do many things. Summer not get hurt if Summer remember to *feel.* Always feel!"

I was mortified that I had so clumsily failed my first lesson. The test received a perfect grade—F. I had wanted to do so good. I had wanted to show her what a great student I would be, how easy things were for me. And I was shot down on the first try. What a low blow to my tender ego.

"Summer angry?"

"Yes, I'm furious with myself."

"What so. You think you smarter than teacher?"

"Of course not!"

"Why Summer so angry about lesson then?"

"Because I failed."

"You no fail, maybe forgot, but no fail. Summer fail if Summer not able to get off couch. Summer go all ways to out there!"

I laughed. "Alright, so I don't get an F, I get a C."

"C good for now. Next time I expect A."

Oh God, this was going to be a lot harder than I had anticipated. Maybe Bill would like to come next time. I'll stay home and babysit.

"*Summer* come. Man come later."

"Alright, you win."

";I no win. What so who win? We do what stuff needed to get Summer ready, that all."

"You're right. I was just fooling around in my head. I didn't actually want Bill to take my place. Although I don't think you would've caught *him* the way you caught me. He always goes with his feelings."

"I know. He make better grade. Summer need work."

"Thanks, I needed that." I was feeling worse.

"Now Summer no understand English. I say Summer need work to be strong for later. Summer main person here."

"I think that didn't help either. I don't want to be a main anything. I just want to be me."

"Nope."

"Nope?"

"Nope. Summer here for me to help on way for later. I do that. You see."

"I give up. Okay, you win."

"No win . . ."

"*No-Eyes, stop!*"

The woman grinned from ear to ear. She had us going around and around on her word game. I realized her joke and joined in the laughter. She spent the rest of the day making me more comfortable with her. We spent some relaxing time on her porch and we spoke of my children. It became easier and easier to be open with her. We spoke of many things that first school day. I had learned a vitally important lesson about truth, about beliefs, about watching, always watching for your feelings.

I hated to leave No-Eyes but was also anxious to get back to Bill. But I wasn't too anxious to tell him how badly I had done on my school lesson, though. I would do better next time, I hoped.

Soul Sight

May Father Sky light all your trails,
And may the Earth Mother keep them
straight.

I reluctantly relived my day with the old woman to Bill.

He laughed at my mistake in observation. He nearly rolled off his chair in hilarious laughter. "That old lady really pulled one over on you. Honey, I think you're going to have to get up awfully early to keep up with her."

Needless to say, I didn't stay up late that night. I was going to be up bright and early—very early.

Under the dark cover of night, our lovely spring turned into a true Rocky Mountain spring. I awoke to a heavy blanket of glistening snow. Damn! I was hoping the unusual balmy weather would continue for a while. Yet, I had experienced too many mountain springs to be actually foolish enough to think the dry days would keep up for very long. Nowhere on earth is Winter as fickle as he is in the Rockies. He is here one day and gone the next. Spring shows her sweet countenance for a week or so, then Winter decides he's not finished and takes another encore. His surprise encores are regular until the stage manager pulls him offstage with his hook around the end of May. I accepted his penchant to ham it up. I had no choice.

I bundled up and was on the lonely roads before dawn. Winter had spread his thick quilt over the newborn aspects of nature. He had brought an etheric quality of hushed silence to my world, a world that

29

was wild with new life just yesterday. I loved the mountains' moodiness. They were forever presenting altered states to the anxious watcher. Surprises were one thing that remained constant and reliable about them. They were forever changing. They were magnificent. And my heart forever belonged to their wild spirit.

The snow was too deep in the narrow road that led to No-Eyes' hill. I parked and trudged in. It was deeper here than I had anticipated. I considered my folly at leaving the well-used snowshoes back in the truck. I labored on. It was cold. The bitterness slapped at my cheeks. By the time I reached the old woman's door my face was red and stiff. My body was thirsty for the flickering warmth of her crackling fire.

She opened the door. "Summer here on time."

I tried to manage a smile, but the corners of my mouth were stiff. I couldn't wait to get in out of the biting wind. Then again, I *had* to wait.

No-Eyes joined me on the porch. She was carrying a long wrapped bundle and motioned for me to follow her. The old woman was nimble for her many years. She made *me* look like the aged one as we trudged through the deep drifts around her cabin. Then again, she was warm from inside the house, while I was waiting for rigor mortis to settle in my frigid bones. I followed her to the crest of the hill.

She worked with an urgency as she surveyed the increasing brightness in the pre-dawn sky. She spoke not a word as she busily went about her preparations.

I watched her kneel and kiss the cold Earth Mother. She was mumbling in a low, reverent tone. She waved me to her side.

I dutifully knelt and followed her every example. I kissed the snow-covered ground. "Bless us and our People, oh Earth Mother. We give thanks for your great gifts and endless bounties." I was becoming warmer. I no longer nurtured the bitter thoughts of cold.

Kneeling on the crest of that high ridge exposed us to the full brunt of the blowing winds. It whipped my scarf away, yet I hardly noticed as the old one's ceremony began to consume the total of my consciousness. Our reverence was complete in this, our magnificent cathedral of the Great Mystery. We knelt in the sacred Presence while the heavens showered us with its crystallized droplets of holy water and the voices on the wind brought a harmonious chorus of sacred chants.

The old one was silent as she looked to me and then bent over her bundle. She reverently removed the elaborately beaded deerskin sheath from the two medicine pipes. Slowly she handed one to me.

I received it as though it was a sacred host being removed from its holy tabernacle.

We stood.

On that blustery crest of the Earth Mother I shivered, not from the winds of winter but from the Presence I felt around us—the glorious Presence of Wakan-Tanka. The great brilliant orb of the rising sun was creeping ever higher to the far snow-capped ridge. I followed every mesmerized movement of the old wise woman. She appeared to be in a private world, a world I readily joined.

Holding the stem end of the pipe skyward, I faced north from whence the winds blow and gave thanks. I then pulled the pipe to my breast. Facing west I again gave thanks. Facing south from whence the warmth comes, I gave thanks. I turned east and gave thanks as the bright circle of the sun broke free over the mountain ridge and sent down its brilliant arrows of light upon our church-on-the-hill. The soft holy flakes gathered on my lashes and melted on the tears on my cheeks. Our timing was perfect. Next, the pipe was held to the Sky Father in thanksgiving. Finally, I lowered it to the ground to show my appreciation for all the Earth Mother had shared with me.

Our morning blessing was concluded. Our Rite of Benediction was over. I was greatly moved. I couldn't find words to properly express my deep emotion over what had just transpired. Two lone women giving thanks, performing an age-old spiritual ceremony—a ceremony not many could ever come close to matching in reverence, not even in the grandest cathedrals of mighty Rome.

We silently replaced the sacred articles back into their receptacle and slowly trudged back to the cabin. Once inside in the homey atmosphere No-Eyes placed the bundles in a special box and we took off our heavy outer wear.

She sat in her rocker and the creak and thud lulled our private musings. The sound served to bind our melancholy thoughts and there we remained for nearly half an hour. The old one broke the stillness with her barely audible whisper. "Summer feel that, huh."

I knew she was referring to my deep emotional state during and after the ceremony. "Yes. It was so incredibly beautiful."

She merely nodded.

I thought I perceived a lone tear coursing down the wrinkled ravine of her cheek. I felt sorry for her lost traditions that were now only a faint memory in an old woman's heart.

"Summer not feel sorry for No-Eyes. Summer feel sorry for Summer. No-Eyes already seen, lived old ways. Summer never seen, never lived that. No-Eyes feel sorry for Summer."

I studied my fingers. She was right. She was so right. I had indeed missed out on a beautiful way of living and believing. I had missed out completely on something that could never be felt or lived again. I then realized her lone tear wasn't for her at all, it was for me.

"We get onto lesson 'fore we no good for nothin'."

I smiled meagerly. She was right. If my saddened mood continued much longer on its present course I wouldn't be in the mood to manage anything.

Outside, the wind blustered the snow into shadowy shapes. It howled for attention as it shook the windows and made the rafters groan. Inside, the comforting fire crackled and made a successful attempt to warm and uplift our spirits. The old woman left her chair and sat cross-legged on the thin braided rug. I followed suit.

"Today Summer learn to see."

I remained silent.

"Peoples all over think they so smart. They think they see all stuff. Humph! They no see *no* stuff. Summer see sometimes. What Summer see?"

I thought a lot before answering. She could be leading into several areas of sight and I wasn't quite sure just which one she meant. I tried an answer, a stab. "The little one."

"Summer see that long ago. Summer afraid that time."

This woman was simply amazing. She knew so many things that were very private—only within the memory of my own mind. She saw things hiding behind the closed doors and in the dark corners of my mind. She knew what crouched and lurked in its shadows. She also saw the locks on some of its doors.

I had referred to something I saw a long time ago, something I saw only once in my entire life, something I desperately had wanted to see again. I will tell you now.

When Bill and I were still high school sweethearts, we took long evening walks. One late afternoon we were in a small park. Bill pushed me on the swings until dusk. We then left the play area and sat down next to a chain-link fence bordering neighborhood yards. Everyone else had left the park and we were completely alone. It was getting darker now. Bill pulled me to him and kissed me. I hugged him. I froze. For behind him, standing in the grass, staring directly at me, was a tiny brown person. It's absolutely true and, no, I'm *not* crazy! I pulled away from Bill and told him I wanted to leave. I was trembling from what I had so suddenly seen. He thought I was chilled and we left the park. I never looked back to the spot to see if the tiny being was still there. I doubt it was. Later I told Bill what had prompted my sudden change in mood. He didn't actually see it but he still believed me all the same. I never ever revealed that incident until now. Some things just aren't possible. Some things just aren't so—unless of course you're ready for the little men in the white coats to come and cart you away where you'll be safe! I wasn't ready for padded walls. I wasn't ready for people to look at me sideways. I wasn't ready to deal personally with what I witnessed. I never got the image of that small being out of my memory. It stayed there, forever imprinted, never spoken about until now. I felt the woman, No-Eyes, would be the one to tell it to. I felt surely she would understand and perhaps be able to explain it to me. I anxiously waited.

Silence.

Perhaps I should've kept it locked in the treasure box of my memory after all. The old one wasn't responding. Perhaps she too was thinking I was nuts.

"Nope. Summer never see one since?"

Instant relief!

"No."

"Summer want to, huh?"

"Yes. Whenever Bill or myself are alone in the woods we want very much to see one. Why haven't we ever seen another one?"

"That not up to Summer or Bill. It up to them."

"Then they *are* real!"

"Yep."

"What *did* I see that day in the park?"

"Special someone, that what. We get to that some other day. That some other lesson. That other stuff."

"I never dreamed anything like that existed. I mean as a child I had picturebooks about fairies and such, but this was really different. It had no wings. It looked like a miniature Polynesian woman with very large round eyes. Her eyes pierced mine with such a depth that she really frightened me."

"Many new things scare. She no mean to scare Summer. She mean to show Summer truth to life. Truth to way things are. She mean to show Summer other side to life. She begin Summer's search."

I thought about that.

"I right?"

"Yes. After that was when I began to go to the library and take out books on the paranormal. The subject intrigued me. I remember now. The little person *was* the very beginning of my search!"

"What else keep it going?"

"What else?"

She simply nodded.

I thought some more. "The ship?"

She again nodded.

Again I will have to backtrack to explain.

All through my childhood I had taken ballet lessons. They began when I was three. My mother played the piano accompaniment for a professional dance school in Detroit. She had no babysitter for me so I went along. All day I watched and participated. These lessons continued long after she stopped playing. When I was a teenager, one night the dance teacher was driving me home from a late-night class. It was dark and we waited in the sidestreet for traffic to clear in order for us to pull out onto the busier main street. Directly in front of us and across the main street was a one-story bank; however, hovering silently above it was an airborne ship of some sort. It had round portholes with yellow light inside, like the kind of light one would see coming from the windows of houses at night. We looked at one another with open jaws. We simultaneously looked back in our rear window to see if the driver of the waiting car behind us saw it too. When we turned to the front again the ship was gone. On the way to my house we hardly spoke at all. We were involved in our private thoughts. I knew she too had seen it. She knew I had seen it. I don't know what she was thinking, but I felt sorry for her. Her husband was a bigwig in the Air Force and I knew that when she told him about it she'd get the usual skeptical reaction. Swamp gas. In the middle of a big city? Smog. On a crystal clear night? Weather balloon. Hovering ten feet above a small bank? Imagination. Simultaneously by two people who were busily discussing other things? Mass hypnosis. When no previous sightings had been reported? No. All the usual standard government explanations were far from plausible in this specific instance. Although, several days after our initial strange experience, the papers were brimming with alleged reports of sightings. Yes, I felt sorry for the reception she would receive that night. Yet, when I excitedly burst through my own door with my fantastic news, I received grins and odd looks. I too was not believed. I stopped raving and went to my room. What was the matter with people? Why didn't they believe? I don't lie. I don't fabricate impossible tales. I merely saw what I saw—we saw.

After that humiliating experience I never again spoke to anyone about my paranormal experiences or about any of the ordinary sightings (which I later had many of in the mountains). People continued to baffle me. I knew because I had seen firsthand. I had read about the government's Blue Book on unusual airborne sightings, yet they too continued to publicly debunk such things, even though many sightings were reported and dutifully recorded by stable and reputable Air Force personnel and sane commercial airline pilots. Were they inebriated? Hallucinating? Given over to misinterpretations of atmospheric conditions? I hardly think so! Yet it remains that alleged scientists and astronomers continue to blatantly display their ignorance by lightly brushing the subject matter off as impossible. Never will I believe they truly do not believe. If they truly do not believe in the physical existence and presence of these airships, then our technology is far less advanced than they would have us believe. I thought our world was advancing forward. Perhaps I am wrong on that count.

Meanwhile, I keep my eyes open and my mouth tightly shut, for I have since seen clusters of these ships in my mountains. Others have too. They too are silent. We know, and I suppose that will have to be enough, for now. The locals know the Rockies are frequented by these air vehicles, but to an outsider: "No. We never seen any." What a pity. It's a damned shame, that's what it is.

Yes, the airship sightings were what No-Eyes was referring to.

I continued the thread of our thoughtful conversation. "Yes, I suppose that ship we saw pushed me further into studying the world's strange occurrences."

"Then what Summer do?"

"Then, the more I read, the more I found out about myself. One subject led to another. Often the material would overlap into another field. I read everything I could get my hands on. Some of the material led into things I considered quite preposterous and I disqualified them. It was fairly simple for me to sort out what was truth, my path. Certain material kept popping up, cross-referencing so to speak. This material stood out like the proverbial sore thumb. It became easy to distinguish my truth from someone's written fantasies."

"Summer still keep quiet?"

"No. By now Bill and I were married and I had shared my paranormal experiences with him. Of course he never was a bit skeptical. How could he be, with living proof? He too had read volumes and had reached the same point as I had."

"That make Summer and Bill happy?"

"Oh no. We were completely alone on a deserted island. Nobody to share it with. We were surrounded by skeptical sharks. Soon we found we couldn't approach anyone on the subject. We were a mated pair bound by our proven beliefs."

"Nobody else?"

"There was one couple. Bill met him at work when he was on afternoons. This man sensed Bill knew certain things. Soon we were meeting at our house late, after they got off work, around one in the morning. His wife began coming over at this same time. We would sit around and do psychic exercises like mind travel. This man told Bill that he was somewhat amazed at the strength of my psychic protection. His words to Bill were, 'It's just like she's sitting in God's hands!' The man himself was very psychic."

"Summer glad of friends?"

"Well, I certainly was at first. It was very exciting to have friends who were of like minds and interests. At least that's what I thought until they wanted to do some things we didn't have an inclination for."

"What that?"

"Dark things."

"What dark thing, Summer?"

"They were real excited about beginning a homesteading community in British Columbia. You know, being secluded away from the maddening crowd when the people went crazy with the earth changes that were coming. Well, this man was a college teacher and they both already had their visas. But it was *how* they were planning on going about it that didn't match our values. They wanted to "see" winning lottery numbers in order to get the money we'd need for the move. Bill and I wouldn't use our senses for things like that. Also, they were into wanting to experiment with things they had read about in the Kabbala and ancient Egyptian writings. Bill and I were definitely not into the mysticism or ceremonial aspect of the paranormal. Our relationship with the couple ended in a kind of psychic battle between Bill and the man. We never saw them again."

"Battle?"

"Yes. The man claimed Bill sent an elemental (thought form) over to hurt him because a vat of hot soup spilled on him. Of course the man retaliated by sending his own elemental into our home. Everyone became very ill. We never suspected what was going on until the man later told us he had sent something over. Anyway, as I said, we never saw them again."

"That because you on different paths right from start."

"That's obvious now. Too bad we didn't see it until after the fact."

"You two still alone?"

"Basically."

"Basically? What *that* 'sposed to mean? What answer that?"

"There's more that I don't want to talk about."

"We no honest here?"

"Yes, we're honest here. It's just that Bill has been the only one I've been able to talk to for so long...."

"*Only* one?"

"I guess you mean Robin."

"Yep."

"You don't miss a trick, do you?"

"Nope."

"Bill met Robin King when they worked together in the Springs. She expressed an intense desire to live the simple life in a mountain cabin. Of course her desire matched that of our own. We eventually became good friends and we invited her to share our cabin in the mountains. Her grasp of our spiritual beliefs was complete. She has made her commitment to our eventual purpose. She desires to be a part of it more than anything. Eventually she married and had a little girl. The marriage didn't work out and she and her child are back with us."

"That crowded?"

"Friends make do. Besides, she is the assistant manager at a convenience store in Woodland. She helps during the day and works at night. We all pull together to get done whatever needs to be done. Actually, we're more like sisters."

"She good friend. She gonna be part of purpose."

"I know."

"Summer know what she gonna do?"

"Not specifically, but I do know that because of her firm commitment she is going to be with us wherever we go."

"Summer go somewheres?"

"Right now it's not feasible."

"*Everything* feasible!"

I sighed.

"Summer give up easy."

I was upset at that quick judgment. "I do *not!* I've tried for seven years to get this material out. I told you before, I'm forever being blocked. We've endured rejections, depressions, loneliness and criticism! Still, here we are pushing ourselves forward. How can you say I give up easy? That wasn't fair and you know it!"

"Maybe, maybe not. Seems to me you think you all done."

"Seems to me we're stuck in a temporary hold, that's all."

"That better way to put it."

I got up and let my legs get better circulation. The fire was dying down and I stirred the hot ashes before adding more logs.

The old woman remained seated on the floor.

I stretched and went to the window. The strong wind had calmed to a gentle breeze, the snow had stopped, and the sun was blinding on the whiteness. It was beautiful but cold. I was thoughtful.

"Summer not happy," she observed.

"No. I'm as happy as I can be, considering. My family has

relatively good health, we have a roof over our heads, food on the table and we have a good friend."

"What so! Summer still not happy."

"How can we really be happy when we've so much to do and no way of doing it? It's damned depressing and frustrating!"

"No have to swear!"

"I didn't."

"*Did!*"

I sighed.

Her tone was soft and sympathetic. "Come sit by me. We talk more."

I supposed I had stretched enough. I sat across from her again.

"Knees no good," she stated.

"And how'd you know that one?"

"No-Eyes see weak spots in aura, here." She pointed to her own bony knees.

"I should've figured that one out for myself."

"Yep. That from dancing?"

"Yep," I teased back.

She grinned. "Glad Summer feel better."

"Glad you're so observant."

She patted my knee. "Summer need something called hope."

"Don't you mean faith?"

"That not same. Faith when someone already believe stuff work out. Hope when someone *not* believe stuff work out—they need hope to keep going."

"Thanks for the clarification. It's kind of a fine line, isn't it?"

"It line all same. We go see something."

"I hope we're going to go right here. It's too cold to go out there."

"Yep."

"Good. I was hoping you'd say that."

"Sit *up!*" she ordered.

The lesson was beginning. I was to learn they always began with her serious businesslike orders. And the eager student always complied.

"Bring up spirit."

I eyed her suspiciously. "Any more tricks? You *are* coming along this time, aren't you?"

"No-Eyes could lead Summer from here, but I come along this time. No trick."

Silence reigned between us until I managed to calm my physical barriers. My mind quieted. My body relaxed as I leaned against the bottom of the couch. My breathing was forcefully deep at first, then shallow and barely audible. I left the physical behind and found the old woman patiently waiting for me.

"Come Summer, we go now to see months ahead."

"The future?"

"Humph! What future? All time one thing!"

I followed her beautiful shimmering form but not until I snuck a quick peek back at the shining glow of my own safety line. Satisfied, I followed No-Eyes outside. We went over the snow-covered trees and were soon speeding over the mountain ranges. I followed her down to a large house. We entered.

"Who you see?"

I froze as I saw myself working at a desk. I was typing a letter.

She grinned wide showing hard pink gums. "Summer have many, many letters to answer."

"From who?"

"Many seekers. This Summer's purpose. This Summer and Bill's future." She left the office room through my library shelves.

I followed and we came upon another office where my friend, Robin, was sitting at a desk piled high with mail. She appeared to be sorting it into separate stacks. The telephone rang and she answered it, "Mountain Brotherhood."

I looked at No-Eyes.

She was leaving again.

I again followed after another glance back at my busy friend.

"This now evening of same day," No-Eyes calmly informed me.

We were in what appeared to be a large family room of the house. A warm fire was blazing in the fireplace. I looked about the room. One complete wall was totally covered with bookshelves. The opposite wall had a long rectangular cupboard with glass doors. Many Kachina dolls were displayed. The room had a warm feeling of comfort to it. Bill, myself, and Robin sat in the soft couches that were arranged in a semicircle in front of the fireplace. Seven other people were sitting with us. It was dark except for the flickering firelight and a few scented candles.

No-Eyes spoke. "Summer listen now."

I did. I listened in on the discussion of the comfortable group of people. The strangers talked of spiritual problems. They asked questions. They were all relating well with one another. I heard No-Eyes' name mentioned. I was telling the group about a lesson I had received. There was added input by Robin. Bill detailed a spiritual concept. It was so beautiful. I felt such a loving sharing going on in that room. I wanted to remain in this warmth forever. The warmth of kindred spirits is like no warmth ever felt. It has a beauty like no beauty ever seen.

No-Eyes nudged my arm. "We go back now."

"No! No, I want to stay awhile."

"Summer get all she need of this soon. We go back now."

She was leaving.

I took one long last look at the beautiful scene of serenity and followed her.

Once outside, she turned to me. "We no need to waste time. Summer think of cabin." She vanished!

I was startled to be left so completely alone. I then remembered what she had told me to do. And no sooner had I thought of her cabin, when I found myself back within the simple structure. I saw her sitting, waiting for me. She had re-entered.

I lowered myself back in and opened my eyes.

"See?" she said confidently, "see how stuff gonna be?"

I was so excited. I had waited so long for just such an actuality. Then a cloud shadowed my vision. "But how far into the future did we go? When was that?"

"Think, Summer!"

How was I to know when that scene was? I didn't know when it was taking place. I felt too excited and confused and scared all at once. If it was too far in the future, that would also be disappointing and just as bad for me in the present to wait for. When it came right down to the bottom line, I was too scared to know the answer to that one.

The wise one urged me on. "Think! Think how you gonna find out when that was!"

"Should we go back?"

"I not go back! Summer want go back alone, Summer go."

I didn't care for that idea at all. In the first place, I didn't know how to get through to a future date. And I certainly didn't care to go it alone either. "No."

"Then Summer look again. Here!" She put a knobby finger to her forehead.

Of course! I could mentally (psychically) view the scene again. I kept my eyes open and stared through No-Eyes.

She was doing the same with me.

I then saw the house again. It had stopped snowing. A full moon bathed the structure in a silvery light. I entered. First the office. It was dark and empty. I peered at the stack of letters on the desk. The moonlight was bright coming through the window in front of it. The stationery had a letterhead. And seeing it made my heart beat faster with anticipation. I glanced over the desk and just before I was about to leave for the other office room I spotted it. And I found what I had come for on the little desk calendar! Immediately my spirit was overjoyed and excited. My sight refocused and I giggled. Now I was back with the old one.

"See how easy?" she bragged.

I was laughing in my state of happiness.

She too crackled a laugh. "Summer use spirit eyes to see stuff, just like No-Eyes. It not so hard."

We got up and I fixed her some tea. The time we had spent on the floor was considerably longer than I had at first realized. The hours had rushed by us. The sun was near setting and I had to be on my way. I hated to leave the brilliant mind of the old one. Her mind was only outshone by the perfect light of her pure spirit.

She spoke of future lesson subject material and outlined our schedule. It would be another week before I could get away again and I knew it would most likely drag by. Already she had worked her good medicine on me. Already I was thirsting for her every wise word.

"Summer not make No-Eyes all important."

"I don't, but you *are* very important."

"Summer have family. Summer needed at home too."

"I know."

"Family appreciate Summer. Summer appreciate family. We be together much enough. What so if Summer not come in week? Summer live and love *all* days. All days new days."

"Yes, that's the kind of thought that has brought us this far."

"Good! I be okay. Summer go now. Summer have many stuff to tell Bill."

I brought in more wood for No-Eyes and wrapped my scarf snugly around my neck. As I was reluctantly getting ready to leave, she hugged me.

"Summer like daughter No-Eyes never have. One day I give memory of old way to Summer."

We hugged longer and I finally tore myself away, but not without tears in my eyes.

Later, after many months of being together, the old Chippewa took me on a mental visit to the old days of the free Indians. She made me feel their emotions. Their happiness was mine. Their colorful ceremonies were mine. Their private thoughts were mine. She instilled a heritage within my heart. She gave me the greatest gift of all time. A gift out of the glorious past. The wondrous gift of a magnificent memory of the way things used to be, but never could be again.

I arrived home well after dark. The kids were long in bed and Bill was reading. He was most anxious to hear of my day and I, in turn, was just as anxious to tell him all I did. That night we fell asleep finally content that the realization of our purpose was actually closer than around the corner. It was visible.

No-Eyes'
Answer

*May you seek after treasures of
precious gold,
And find them within the hearts of
others.*

Today was going to be one of my special days. I was going to
spend it with No-Eyes. I was filled with a great anticipation as I wheeled
our old Chevy pickup into the end of the road below her cabin. I would
have to walk to reach her house and each step served to intensify my
excitement. As I picked my way through the early morning's rolling
mist, I secretly imagined what possible or, more accurately, impossible
places she would lead me to, through, and safely back from again. I
paused to squint up to the sun as its spirit wafted lazily about the
woods, meandering here through waking aspen stands and there
between fallen pines. I thanked the Sun Spirit for all her life-giving aid
to all things alive and growing. A lark bunting swept gracefully past me
as if to signal me that I was dallying far too long. The momentary
thought crossed my mind that I was indeed keeping the old Chippewa
woman waiting and that I must hurry along so as not to shorten our
productive day together. Then I chuckled to myself as I checked my
quickened pace. Certainly I knew the old woman better than that. She
was not one to wait for anyone. She was constantly busy in or around
her cabin. It would almost seem as though nobody or nothing could
hurry her or cause her even the slightest twinge of anxiety. I would like
to think that my recent periodic visits meant more to her than an
ordinary day alone; however, I don't think any of the old woman's days

are ordinary, at least not by any measurement of modern man's standards of comparison. I just never knew what to expect and that was the most exciting part for me.

As I neared her cabin, the natural pandemonium of forest sounds became suddenly quiet. It was so still even the trees appeared to be merely paintings upon some unseen artist's canvas. This was a real new one on me. I wasn't sure what I should do. Always before, everything was cheerful and busy around her house, but this, this was downright spooky.

I could feel the tiny beads of moisture seeping their way out of my pores, and the subtle pricking sensation of the hairs on my neck pulsed the familiar message of warning flashing to my brain. Usually when I would have these aberrant sensations I would know that I was in the unseen presence of something other than good. Sometimes I could immediately recognize and identify its source and I would take appropriate measures to deal with it. Other times, like now, when I couldn't put my finger on the presence, I would always slowly back away from it until the negative sensations were completely gone. This time, however, I didn't back away. I felt drawn to the old woman's quiet cabin. I felt as though I was moving on numb and paralyzed limbs, yet somehow I was moving forward. My awful warning signals persisted. My mind could not comprehend why I wasn't turning tail and racing madly away from this horrible vortex of terror causing such inner fear. I continued to slowly advance toward the house. I was now at the cabin steps and I knew my legs were raising, one timeless step at a time.

My mind was now in such a horrified state of confusion I felt no more bodily sensations and gave over to a total and complete submission to whatever was causing such willful power. I gave in to it and I miraculously felt an elation I've never felt before or since. I opened the rickety door and entered.

For such a bright and sunny day outside, the small interior of the cabin was dark with a smoky, wavering sort of darkness. I had to take some minutes for my eyes to make their needed adjustment. No-Eyes was calmly sitting in her motionless rocking chair, eyes closed and stone still. My heart gave a painful surge. I thought the old woman was dead. She didn't move when I softly called to her and I crept across the room to kneel down near her. I gently touched her veined hand. It was cold. I could hear no audible breathing and I peered with held breath into her time-wrinkled face.

Suddenly, No-Eyes snapped open one wide ebony eye and a sly grin crept up the corners of her mouth. I jumped back in total shock and fell off balance onto the hard pine floor.

44

"Summer sound like she seen dead someone, huh Summer?"

I was in a quagmire of mixed and jumbled-up emotions. I didn't know whether I should get up and immediately proceed to strangle No-Eyes for scaring me so bad or whether I should hug her for not being dead. I sat where I had fallen and stared at her until my feelings were properly sorted out.

Her old impaired rocker began its rhythmic creak and thud, creak and thud. The birds were again breaking out in their raucous fighting over scraps of food. The warming breeze played with her thin, tattered curtains. I took all this normalcy in, but what soothed my flaming anger the most was her infectious grinning. Who could ever be angry at an old woman with twinkling eyes and a toothless grin? I conceded, shook my head, and grinned back at her.

Even though No-Eyes was totally blind, I knew she had a unique way of seeing everything she needed or wanted to see. She had seen me enter the still clearing around her house. She had seen my zombie-like approach and, worst of all, she had seen my sudden fright when she cleverly whipped open that one sightless eye of hers. I was naturally embarrassed and deeply mortified at having been the object of her questionable humor. Yet, No-Eyes never wasted her precious time or her valuable energies unless some vital lesson was involved. This I had come to learn just as I was to learn her special way of seeing without using my eyes.

"No-Eyes, I hope you enjoyed your fun. Now that you've had a good laugh on me, what in God's name did I pass through out there?" I excitedly asked of her.

As No-Eyes got out of her chair, I could almost hear the creaking of her brittle bones. She shuffled to the window, looked to the sun, and turned to me. "Summer felt answer to Summer's question," she replied so matter-of-factly.

Oh boy, was I mixed up. I hadn't asked her any questions and I couldn't for the life of me connect anything I would've said to those horrid and vile vibrations I had passed through. I could've sworn that some great embodiment of evil was going to powerfully devour me at any instant. I've felt it before, but never before have I purposely approached it, much less passed through it. I just couldn't make the proper connections that No-Eyes was inferring were there to make. I must have looked like a stupid schoolgirl to her because she sure had a way of making me feel like one.

I flopped down on the threadbare couch and sort of pouted. No-Eyes had her eyes closed as she faced the far mountain range. We stayed that way, frozen in time, for I don't know how long. Suddenly one of my most recent questions popped into my mind; more than likely she was putting it there. She was good at making one feel her own thoughts were really theirs. I broke the silence between us. "No-Eyes, did all that funny business outside have anything to do with what I asked you about people and why they aren't sensitive to nature?" I asked sheepishly.

She grinned and nodded.

Silence reigned once again and set the mood for deep thought. I became contemplative while I desperately tried to sort out what it all meant. I didn't see how she had given me any real answer at all. This one was a real doozey. A real mental maze for me to feel my way through.

Sometimes communicating with No-Eyes could be a real mental challenge in logic. I thought about it some more. I was getting absolutely nowhere. If a viable and logical connection did exist between my innocent question and the horror I felt outside, it was totally lost to me. This one, I couldn't figure out on my own. I guess I needed many, many more lessons.

She sat down next to me and reached for my hand. She patted it and enclosed both of hers around mine. "Summer," she began softly, "you want know so many things, yet Summer must learn to see clear."

I released an affirmative sigh and listened for the wise words I knew were to follow.

"I bring Summer all bad feeling of others. I show Summer what in hearts of ones who cannot see Great Spirit in all things. Summer scared those bad feelings, but Summer okay, huh."

The corny lightbulb flashed stupidly on and off in my head. Of course, that was the solid connection!

Our involved conversation continued long into the early afternoon as my lesson commenced in full swing. No-Eyes told me that she needed an impressionable way to show me the answer to my question. In my opinion, as if that held any water with her, she could've picked something a little less frightening. But such were the old woman's teaching ways—ways that one never forgot.

She told me that if she could make my spirit feel, actually feel, what the wants and desires were of most people, I would then understand why those same people are so insensitive to the spirit and beauty of nature. I would then understand why they fear a mountain night and why they do not even see the flowers, much less stop along the wayside to rejoice in their sweetness of scent.

She patiently explained to me that what I sensed and feared was their misplaced purpose-of-life. I felt greed for wealth and position. I sensed the dog-eat-dog attitude of stabbing your neighbor in the back if it will be to personal advantage. I felt hundreds of lies and falsehoods, jealousy and envy, hate heaped upon vengeful hate heaped upon murderous hate. I felt anger, an incredible anger. I felt the terrifying total absence of God.

No-Eyes completely explained all these fearsome feelings I sensed and she also explained that even though I was as scared as I was, I was able to pass through them unharmed because I myself had no possession of them. I was removed and untouchable, so to speak.

She explained that if I had even secretly harbored any one of those negative feelings within my heart, then I would surely have been seriously affected. I was able to walk through the terrible psychic vortex only because I possessed entirely opposing desires, wants, and feelings.

I kindly thanked her for her explicit answer but hinted that she not be so graphic the next time.

She squeezed my hand and we finished the day busily restocking her medicinal supply. No-Eyes is truly one of the greatest medicine women of her time. She had potions and concoctions that would rival any modern-day pharmaceutical company. She has stores of bottles, jars, vials, and boxes filled with all manner of mysterious things. She is a wonderfully sweet woman who has tightly grasped the lost understanding of the old ways of healing. She knows every plant, where it can be found, what it can do for you, and when it should be picked for proper potency. No-Eyes told me she would teach me some of these things if I had the inclination to learn of them. I do.

She possesses a great amount of patience and understanding. She has a certain way of making you think out your own questions in a logical pattern. No-Eyes has no sight, yet the very loving aura of God radiates from her aged being.

As the fingers of sunlight became longer and longer, I knew it was time for me to leave this warm and wonderful place of learning. We had spent a happy day talking and sorting out her bottles. I held No-Eyes' old hands tenderly between my own. No words were necessary.

When I went to leave, I paused at her open doorway and peered out. She called to me, "They gone, Summer, they all go away."

I turned back to her in time to hear a slight chuckle behind that wonderful toothless grin. I confidently left the old woman's place. The walk to my truck was comforting as the dusky light filtered in around me. The little woodland inhabitants were hurriedly getting ready for bed and as I started the engine I looked through the trees and saw No-Eyes standing on her porch. She faced the glorious setting sun, raised her thin arms up, and gave thanks. Perhaps she was thanking the Great Spirit for the beautiful warm day. Perhaps she was giving thanks for one more day of life allotted to her. Or perhaps she was giving thanks that my path has crossed hers. I'd like to believe that.

The Gift of Wakan-Tanka

May your mind shimmer with the
glow of Truth,
And may your Spirit guard its
sacred ground.

The late spring snows eventually gave way to a spectacular summer. The Earth Mother left nothing out. The sun was warm and touched all of life with rays of happiness. One immensely enjoyable aspect of the Colorado Rockies are the many days of sunshine. Nearly every day, winter included, is basked in the glorious bright sunshine. The gray skies of the east are indeed a rarity here.

Summer was upon us in full swing and so were the tourists. Our little town on the mountain pass was bumper-to-bumper with all manner of vacation vehicles. On any given day you could count half of the United States represented on the license plates cruising through our main street. I used to hate all the fair-weather intruders. That is, until I came to the realization that the magnificence of the mountains was here for all to see and enjoy. I don't mind the tourists so much any more.

I enjoyed summer. Although autumn was my favorite season, summer was the only time I could reach for the sun. I would sit on our deck for hours soaking in its unlimited energies. No-Eyes had instructed me on the finer aspects of sunbathing without having any ill effects of the radiating rays. Never did I lay out between the hours of eleven in the morning and two in the afternoon. She always cautioned that between two and four were the best times for a deeper tan. It all had to do with the slant of the sun's rays. Of course, knowing No-Eyes, there had to be more to it than just plunking yourself down in a lounge chair. And there was more.

She told me that I had to reinforce my bodily protection, put up a shield, so to speak. Mentally, this shield acted as a glass window between myself and the harmful radiation. I learned to talk to the sun as I enjoyed its warmth permeating my entire body. "Oh, Great Being of the Sky Father, I am ever thankful for your healthful rays. Enter this body and grant it your bountiful energies. May only your healthful rays touch this thankful body."

And I learned to talk to my body. No-Eyes forever stressed how it was that the mind alone could control the health or the illness of the physical body. Positive, good, optimistic, and loving thoughts were the main ingredients to health. As above (mind) so below (physical body). I talked to my physical while sunbathing. "Let in no harmful rays. Only allow the healthful and healing energies in to energize and equalize all the system's total balance. Only healthful healing rays may enter. All harmful rays *must* reflect back off my shield." This liturgy was repeated many times as I layed out in the beautiful being of the sun. Many times I caught myself smiling as I said the words. It was such a good feeling. I could almost perceive the sun's healthful rays entering my body and healing various less-than-healthy areas. And indeed, I did visualize such a therapeutic energy treatment. My daily sunbathing was treated like a rest from the pace of the world. There I could rest and let the body's systems become totally revitalized with the powerful force of the sun.

I was taking my usual route to the old woman's cabin. I was fortunate I didn't have to contend with the massive conglomeration of travel trailers, as my trail was rarely used by others. I was in exceptionally high spirits this lovely morning. Even though it was still early with the pre-dawn grayness, I could tell the day was going to present another one of her masterpieces. I was full of Rocky Mountain highs lately. My spirit soared with so many things to be thankful for. I had three beautiful daughters, a wonderful friend who just so happened to also be my husband, and all four were happy and vitally healthy. I had my own health, food on our table, a modest roof over all our heads, and a true friend. And I had No-Eyes. I was incredibly happy this morning. I thought about the ceremony No-Eyes and I would perform. It was going to be something special—it always was. I had come to look forward to our ritual of dawn's greeting. It was a prayer of thanksgiving. It was something beautiful.

My mental musings had slowed me down. I hurried up No-Eyes'

hill when I saw her reaching its crest. No longer was it cold and snow-covered. Now a multitude of wildflowers offered up their pleasing incense in our sacred cathedral. We performed the morning rite and walked back to the cabin. Now I was allowed to carry the sacred bundle.

"Do we have to go inside?" I asked as we neared the cabin.

She stopped her rhythmic stride. "You gonna hold those all day?"

"No. Can we put these away and come back out? It's going to be a beautiful day."

She humorously sniffed at the air that was heavy with nature's fine essence. She lifted her brown face to the eastern sun, its weak rays already becoming stronger. She looked to me. "Summer, put those up. We stay out today."

I ran into the cool cabin and reverently set the two medicine pipes in their box. I rejoined her outside in the sun.

She had pulled up two of the old chairs made from aspen branches. She patted the seat of one.

I sat facing her. "Going to be just gorgeous today, No-Eyes. You should see all the tourists in town. Looks like a Shriners' convention." I laughed.

"Look like what?"

I realized she didn't know what a Shriner was. "Well . . ."

"What so! I no like crowds. I no need to know this."

"Okay. You're the boss here."

She rested back in her stiff chair and sighed.

I didn't particularly like those hard chairs. "Is it alright if I sit in the grass?"

"No matter."

I moved the crooked chair aside and sat cross-legged in front of her.

"That no good."

"What do you mean? You just said I could sit in the grass!"

"Summer no more sit that way—bad for no-good knees. Summer need pressure this way." She demonstrated with her own knees. "Before sleep, Summer need to keep right knee bent out—so pressure here. You see? Pain go away then."

I followed her suggestion. I slept the way she told me to and the cartilage in my right knee never again moved around and clicked when I walked.

"This good day for love lesson."

That sounded in keeping with the type of day. It was lovely.

"Summer gonna listen or have birds sing in ear?"

I grinned. "I'm going to listen."

"Good!"

"Are we going anywhere today?"

"Maybe, maybe not. We see how lesson gonna go."

I was watching a peregrine falcon sail effortlessly over his azure ocean.

"We gonna go inside! Summer no one mind today. Mind all over mountains!"

"No. I'm sorry. I'm listening."

Silence. She was checking.

"See? I *am* listening," I assured.

"Humph!"

It appeared to me that the old one wanted to rock. She always rocked when she was giving a lesson. "You want me to go and get your rocker? I could bring it out he. . . ."

"*Summer!* How No-Eyes *think* with Summer's mouth going all time? Huh?"

"I just thought. . . ."

"I think! Summer *listen!*"

"You don't have to get all worked up. I was just trying to. . . ."

"Listen?"

"No. But now I will. I promise."

"Humph. Took Summer long enough to learn listen lesson, Summer remember that one?"

Boy! Did I ever remember that one, how could I ever forget it? It damned near killed me! "I remember," I answered sheepishly.

"Good! We get going now. We gonna talk 'bout love. Not lovers' love—just love, emotion love."

I was listening.

"Our Peoples have real love. They know what love was, have a spirit movement—a special vibration, here." She pointed to her heart. "Long ago Peoples not think of themselves like peoples today. Love *never* for self. Love for other peoples—always. Our Peoples know love and Great Mystery be one thing. This important, Summer."

I reassured her. "I'm here. I'm listening. I love it when you talk about the old ways."

"*Not* old ways. These ways still good *now*. That what wrong. Peoples now not live old ways! I speak 'bout old *days* when People love right—in heart."

"I get it. Go on."

She sighed.

A gentle breeze rustled through the tall aspens. Kaibab squirrels scampered playfully under the nearby squawberry bushes. Birds raucously chirped and hopped from one branch to the next, shaking the emerald aspen leaves. A curious porcupine waddled out from under a fallen log. Butterfly wings reflected an ever-changing kaleidoscope of transparent colors as they flitted around the tall golden banners. The flowers themselves nodded and swayed in time with the wind's gentle tune. No-Eyes made her words sparkle with expressive animation. The sky had been painted in dazzling pigments of azure and cerulean, it was a masterful backdrop for my pastoral setting. God, it was hard to sit still. I suffocated the gypsy in my wandering spirit. It desperately desired to dash up the deep green crest of the ridge and take off in a wanton flight with the high-flying falcon. I loved the innocent beauty of nature. I loved my mountains. I loved their pristine character. Suddenly I realized the old woman wasn't talking any more and I didn't know when she had stopped. I was in big trouble. I kept my head down and strained my eyes up to her face. Lord above, the old lady was asleep! I then looked up full at her.

No-Eyes let one lazy eyelid raise. She was looking right at me.

"I thought you were asleep," I said.

"Might as well be. Summer sleeping—up here!" she replied, pointing to her temple.

I was sincerely sorry for mentally drifting off the way I so rudely had done. I was ashamed for not paying attention to the old woman's words. What could I say? Nothing.

"Now Summer gonna study hands? No find answer there."

I remained mortified.

"Summer stop feeling bad. Summer just show big part of lesson."

A flutter of relief came through my spirit. "How? How was I doing a part of your lesson?"

"Humph. When Summer gonna learn to put parts into one?" She sighed. "What Summer feel when I talking?"

I didn't want to admit what I had been feeling. I was supposed to be listening, not feeling. Yet through her wise knowledge, I knew better than to ever attempt to lie to her. "I was thinking how much I loved the mountains. Everything is so full of a wild life! I was watching the falcon soar and dive. I noticed how the sun reflected through the colors of the thin butterfly wings. And the kaibabs, they were having the most marvelous time with their game of tag! The wind blew her breath through the aspens and they quivered like...."

The old Chippewa was grinning wide.

I laughed with the realization. Of course! I had become completely consumed with my love of nature. Love, that's what my lesson was all about—a selfless love.

Together we shared the merriment of the incident.

"Summer no just listen. Summer do! That fine, I not angry."

I expressed my relief, yet also told her I was still ashamed for not paying better attention to the subject at hand. I would certainly have to control my emotions more. I had a terrible weakness for giving in to them.

"We go on. Ready now?"

I nodded, convinced I would gain a firm hold on my desire to watch nature.

"Now, in old days Peoples love all stuff. They love trees, mountains, grass, animals, all stuff. Sacred powers were nature forces: wind, water, fire, lightning. Peoples know Father Sky and Earth Mother parents of all life. Every creature have spirit. All nature be People's church. It be bad stuff to force Great Spirit to crouch down into one building. Great Spirit everywhere! It forever duty of Peoples to every day give prayers to Great Mystery, to be thankful. These prayers more important to Peoples than food even. All Peoples see Great Spirit in black rainclouds, hear Him in thundering waterfalls. Peoples make all acts in life a sacred act. Peoples know sacred silence is voice of Great Spirit. This silence be ultimate balance of mind, body, and spirit. Peoples give away all one's stuff! They know stuff not where Great Spirit be. Stuff not important! Summer, that true love. That pure love!"

"It's beautiful. Too bad the people of today can't bring themselves to do that."

"Too bad? Why not?"

I laughed. "People think they need their personal things. They think the more they've acquired, the more successful they are and others will admire that success. That makes them feel good. They could never part with their things."

"Stuff puff them up like stinking buffalo dead on dry prairie."

"That just about says it all, No-Eyes."

"Peoples need to see they no can love that way. They need to see how they do all stuff for self. Self have to go first—then pure love can come into hearts. In old days Peoples give all stuff away to other Peoples. They no love stuff. They only love other Peoples, Earth Mother, and Great Mystery."

I felt bad. "No-Eyes, people today are too worried about methods of gaining more material possessions than their neighbor. It's a sort of preoccupation with them. It's a constant battle for most and best and biggest. People would be lost without their things."

"Not Bill and Summer."

"That's a lot different."

"How that so different?"

"You know."

"Tell No-Eyes how you so different."

"Circumstances. We've always had it hard. Bill worked for thirteen years in one company. He worked his way up to where we didn't have to tighten our belts all the time and then they went on a long strike. It lasted a very long time. We sold his rifles and my wedding rings. We had three little girls to feed. Life was always one unending teeter-totter ride, up one week and down the next. We just always did whatever was needed to do in order to survive. That was life for us. Nothing more, nothing less."

"Other peoples sell stuff too."

"Do you really think they'd actually sell their diamonds?"

"What so 'bout diamonds! What they anyways? They not mean love. They only sign. Peoples not need diamonds to show they mates!"

"No-Eyes, I know that and you know that, but it's tradition."

"Blah! Peoples need to see better."

"Regardless, they don't. I don't think they ever will either. Some things just don't change, No-Eyes. If they do, it takes a very long, long time."

"Things change anyways. Things gonna change for all peoples that love stuff."

"No-Eyes, things will change for everyone." The discussion was becoming serious now.

She nodded.

I knew that if the old one was in her rocker right now, it'd be creaking and thudding to a furious pace. She always rocked faster when her dander was up.

"Peoples better get going. They better stop loving stuff now. Peoples' stuff gonna be no good later."

"No-Eyes, a lot of people don't believe things are going to change."

"What so! They gonna find out how good stuff be when they no have food in house, in store even! Then they can eat their great stuff. They gonna find out how great stuff be when they no can get gas! They gonna find out but good. What they gonna do with great stuff when crazy peoples running all over? What so 'bout no electricity, no natural gas, no propane? Huh Summer, what so then?"

I could see she was really upsetting herself. I'd never seen her so worked up. She continued ranting.

"Peoples *stupid!* They no have eyes, no brain even! Time come when they be shooting peoples for food even. Peoples be *dumb!*"

She was trembling.

"No-Eyes, please calm down. We're not concerning ourselves with those people who aren't listening or are skeptical. We only need to reach the ones who know and believe. We need to reach the ones who don't know but *will* believe. Those others will never be convinced because they don't want to be. They have all kinds of selfish excuses for not believing."

"That only cheap coverup!"

"Of course it is, but they would never admit to that either. No-Eyes, we're here to help and comfort those who seek those things. We're not here to convince the skeptic. There's no more time left for that, besides, I don't care about the skeptics anyway."

"Summer have to care 'bout *all* peoples."

"I'm sorry, No-Eyes, but I've gone through too much to waste time on the unbelievers. Time is getting too short. Things are too close now."

"It no waste of time. Summer need to convince."

"Not anymore I don't. Between my months with you and my years with Bill's guide, I've found out that it *is* a waste of time and energy to take the time with those with closed eyes and ears and hearts. Their spirits haven't come far enough."

Silence.

"Did you hear what I said?"

"Summer ready to talk 'bout that guide now?"

"Not yet, No-Eyes. I'm not sure I'll ever be. It's been a very personal thing between us. I think we'd best leave him out of this. At least until I feel the right time has come—not yet."

"Summer think No-Eyes in dark?"

"That's not what I said at all. I suppose you know all about him, how he came, when he came and why. Yet, I'm not prepared to discuss that."

"Not prepared or not *want* to."

"Probably both."

"Humph. Okay Summer, maybe some other time, later."

"Yeah, maybe later. Thanks for understanding."

"Humph."

Although she appeared to understand my personal position on the private subject, she pushed a little further.

"Summer want No-Eyes to tell 'bout him?"

"*No-Eyes!* Please!"

"We have to speak 'bout it sooner or later. Summer know that!"

"Yes, but not just yet."

"Okay. We get back to love."

"Fine."

"Love have to be in heart before peoples can live with Great Spirit. Great Spirit big part of peoples love. They need to see Great Spirit in heart. They need to know Great Spirit part of people's spirit. It all one! If peoples get rid of stuff, they see and hear Great Spirit in other peoples. No can share and live good without seeing and hearing. People block love out with too many stuff and bad feelings. Bad feelings always keep love away. The Peoples, our Peoples always love all nature stuff, all other Peoples. Our People see and hear Great Spirit in all stuff of nature."

"You mentioned bad feelings. You meant things like hate, jealousy, and greed, didn't you?"

"Yep. These feelings make body sick even. Bad feelings make body not balanced. Bad feelings bring up dark force in body. Thoughts real stuff. All bad thoughts make body acid with disease. Body needs no acid condition. Systems not good balance in acid. It way off kitter."

"You mean off *kilter.*"

"What so! Summer know what meant."

"I'm sorry."

"What so. I not always speak right word. I always speak right thought. Summer know what No-Eyes speak is right. Summer already know these things, huh?"

"Yes, but I like hearing how our People lived right, how they loved their precious land, how they gave unselfishly to each other. I wish things were like that today. Everything is so hurried through, even eating is rushed."

"Peoples today not know how to eat even. They not know how bad feelings upset eating systems. They wonder then why some stuff not agree. They eat too fast. They eat when angry and sad even. They eat when not hungry even. They all dumb!"

"Well, you can't just make them change overnight."

"They *never* change!"

"Maybe not."

"Humph. Peoples stupid, that all. We go somewheres."

"Where?"

"Wakan-Tanka give Peoples many good stuff, love one great stuff. He give special sight of observation, too. No-Eyes show Summer that one. Bring up spirit."

If I was going to leave my body behind, I had to get into a more relaxed position. I lay in the noonday shade of the tall aspens. My breathing softened. I felt the usual dizzy sensation of my brain's alpha waves. Soon I felt peace. I was out.

No-Eyes, as always, was waiting patiently for me. She could be out at the snap of a finger. I was getting better.

"Come Summer, we join falcon."

The beautiful bird was still riding the winds of the valley. We drifted to its side. We joined its silent flight. Up we soared and down we dived. It was our unique way of having some fun. It was our way of sharing a special peace, a momentary hiatus from our heavy lessons. If I could only explain the magnificent sensation of being free of the terrible heaviness of the physical body. I wish with all my heart that I could properly convey this wondrous, weightless freedom. The astronauts don't even come close, for they still are clumsily fettered by complicated suits, they bump into objects. They have barriers that we do not. If only the English language provided me with appropriate adjectives to describe the feeling. Magical, wonderful, unique, spectacular are so incredibly mundane. They sorely lack meaning. I wish all people would realize their spirit's capacity to do this. To ride the wind and join a falcon was truly a great gift of heritage from the Great Spirit.

No-Eyes was back.

I didn't want to leave the mighty falcon; then again, my purpose was to learn. I re-entered and opened my eyes. "Why'd we come back?"

"We go again."

"Good." I closed my eyes.

"From *here!*"

"Here? I can't fly from here!"

"Summer gonna! Summer gonna learn."

Oh God, it was such a gorgeous day. Why did I have to waste it working so hard?

"Summer not waste! Summer *need* to travel from here." She motioned to her head.

"Alright." I got more comfortable in the grass.

"Sit up."

"But I'll fall if I leave."

"Summer not gonna leave. Summer stay in body."

"I thought you said I was going to travel?"

"Only up in head, Summer, only in head."

Since I wasn't allowed to cross my legs any more, I pulled up the hard chair and sat in it. I moved around until I was fairly comfortable.

"You like worm."

I smiled. "Well, these chairs aren't exactly the most comfortable things in the world." I squirmed again.

"No-Eyes not wait all day!"

"Alright, I'm ready, I think."

She knew I was teasing. I was ready.

"We gonna watch beavers down there."

A small stream coursed by the bottom of No-Eyes' hill. It was inhabited by an industrious family of beavers. We could ever be aware of their incessant splashing. I watched the beavers. I watched their busy antics.

"Summer not only watch. Summer observe."

I observed. The more I silently observed, the more intense my concentration was becoming. I became totally absorbed in the furry animals' activities. I found I wasn't aware of anything other than the beaver's world. The senses were picking up a fine essence. I felt the prickly dry grass. The grasses smelled sweet, a scent of clover drifted through my nostrils. The weight of wet fur was cumbersome. The sound of gnawing on fresh young aspenwood was loud in my ears. Wet fur was being shook dry. "This is wonder. . . ." I no longer was among the beavers, but back in the hard chair on the hill. "What happened?"

"Summer stop observing, that what. Summer remember self. No can observe and be aware of self at same time. Summer have to forget self. Now, go back."

I once again began observing. I had to forget I was a physical separate entity, an entity separate from the subject of my observations. Now that I knew what I was supposed to be doing, it was easier. Soon I was back down with the beavers. I was one with them. It was like having my consciousness move from me to them. I was here in a chair, yet my mind was not. The mind had traveled, through observation, to a point designated by the conscious. Again I was one with the beaver family. The swift, running stream waters were cold, yet the thick fur was successfully insulating against the wet chill. Small particles of mica and pyrite glistened with the reflected sunlight on the streambed. It was an enjoyable sensation to move through the gurgling waters; the sound was muffled from below the surface of ripples. Echoes of the ripples were reverberating off the underwater boulders. The mass of sticks, mud, and branches was huge. The water was still on this side of the expertly engineered dam. A small opening was directly in front.

"*Summer!*"

My mystical adventure was rudely interrupted just as I was about to enter the interior of the dam. "Why'd you do that? I was just about to see what their home was like!"

"Great Spirit give gift of observation to learn, not pry."

"Pry! They're just beavers, No-Eyes, not people!"

"They peoples to them. Summer go into peoples' private rooms?"

"That's a silly question. Of course not!"

"*All* creatures Great Spirit's children. All creatures need privacy too. All creatures have feelings."

I thought about that. I knew the animals had feelings. I knew they had their own unique ways of communicating. Yes, they were very much like people.

"Well?"

"You're right. I shouldn't pry."

"That gift special. No use it to pry. It easy to misuse. Summer no misuse."

"No. I wouldn't do that and you know it."

"Yep. I know. Just wanna make sure Summer know."

I grinned.

"Too bad peoples not know secret to see stuff."

"No-Eyes, I think it's a good thing they don't know. Just think how they'd use it."

"*Misuse!*"

"Yes."

"It shame. Peoples got many heritage gifts from Great Spirit. They not even know how rich they be."

"Wouldn't it be a beautiful place to live if everyone knew and used them for good? Just think how the world would advance. Technology would be used for peace instead of for war."

"War, yes. That coming."

"I know." Why did we forever have to get into these awfully depressing subjects?

"Summer no worry. They not gonna let it get far." She pointed to the sky.

"I know."

"How Summer know?"

"Remember? I'm not ready to talk about that yet."

"That? Summer mean him."

"Yeah, him."

"What so, anyways. Peoples gonna know 'bout him someday."

"Maybe, maybe not."

"Why maybe not, Summer?"

"Why? Because too many books are out about spirit guides talking through people. The things they've supposedly said are absurd! That's why. And I'm not going to be classed with them. We've been getting things from God's right-hand man. I'm just not going to expose myself any further than I already have. Subject *closed!*"

"Almost."

"What's that supposed to mean?"

"Closed for now, that all."

"Wrong. It's closed for good! At least as far as the public is concerned. It's nobody's business but ours."

"Who? Robin know 'bout him?"

"Yes, but only because she's in the group."

"Who else speak to her?"

"The other one—her guide."

"Okay. We not speak more—yet."

"Do you always have to have the final word?"

"Yep."

"Then tell me, what good would it do to have everyone know?"

"Peoples believe Summer tell truth. Peoples seeking that truth."

"*You* speak the truth. Why should I have to prove I too speak the truth? I don't like the smell of this."

"It no have smell. Many seekers looking for truth."

"I know, but I already told you how strongly I feel. I'm *not* about to go around knocking myself out trying to convert skeptics, trying to convince people. No-Eyes, people feel it within their hearts when they come across the truth. It's as simple as a personal awakening, a spirit's private recognition!"

"Summer stubborn."

"I'm *not* stubborn! I'm just not going to go around baring my soul to the world; half of them don't believe anyway."

"That where Bill and Summer come in. That where Mountain Brotherhood come in."

"Oh no. You're not going to bring me into that one, no way!"

"We see, Summer, we see. Some stuff Summer have no say."

"No-Eyes," I said softly, "we're very tired, too tired. We've sought truth. We found it. We're learning more from you. We desperately need to be alone. Can't you see the peace we need now?"

Silence.

I knew the old woman saw the peace we needed. She knew how long and difficult our path had been. She knew things I never told her. It was obvious how she knew private matters. No-Eyes was cognizant to the wiles of nature. She knew that all things were possible because she had personally broken through so many of the "impossibilities" of science. She had peered through the darkened windows of the universe and seen the other side. She had opened the locked doors of science and slowly stepped over their threshold. Because of her patient perseverance, I was brought to these same windows and doors. Yet, although we two women would appear to be like-minded, we had one forbidding stumbling block. This would arise now and again during our many discussions. Each one adamant. Each one sure of her convictions and the final outcome. I held my ground. Some aspects of our searching must be left private. I speak of one fruit of that search. I maintain that merely because I have shared my lessons with the wise Chippewa with you, the reader, this in no way obligates me to share everything. Some aspects remain too private, and because of this, I firmly hold my ground, a ground that is incredibly sacred.

No-Eyes' Marketplace

May you tread softly upon the Earth Mother's breast,
And may you be ever thankful for her endless bounties.

The town of Woodland Park, Colorado is situated on a mountain pass. It is nestled between two ranges that are covered with tall, thriving pines and aspens. Pikes Peak is boldly visible from every viewpoint of the town. It is a quiet place; however, it is growing larger by the week.

Every Saturday, Bill and I drive uptown to a quaint little restaurant called Godmother's Kitchen. The owners, Helen and Elmer, are two of the nicest folks you'd ever want to know. They are gracious enough to let me sit in one of their corner booths several times a week and work on my notes.

One brilliant summer morning, when the restaurant was bursting at its seams with tourists, Bill began commenting on how much he loved Elmer's pancakes. "There's no place in town that dishes up a breakfast comparable to Elmer's," he'd say. That thought brought me to thinking about No-Eyes. If she were with us, I wondered what she would've asked for in her omelet. I then told Bill about my old friend's uncommon larder of food. He listened with attentive interest as I told him how I came to be acquainted with her unusual pantry.

On one particularly clear summer day, I visited No-Eyes at her cabin. The massive lodgepoles around my parking area were laughing with delight as the sun tickled their high bottlebrush branches. The chickadees were chirping gaily and the kaibab squirrels were actively engrossed in a very serious game of tag. All the woodland creatures were taking exceptional joy in the beautiful, balmy mountain morning. My heart sang with happiness as I approached her door and stepped within the cool, dark interior.

"Summer eat?" she questioned from her kitchen.

"Oh, yes, I already had breakfast. Thanks anyway."

She nodded and continued puttering about her pantry.

Nobody spoke.

I made myself comfortable on her sofa and tried to wait patiently for our day to begin. It was extremely difficult for me to have patience when I was with No-Eyes. Nevertheless, I waited in silence while I gave her meager cabin a more thorough inspection.

The cabin largely consisted of one main room. The living area boasted a moss rock fireplace, which was well utilized; her rickety rocker, one frayed upholstered chair, an old table with a radio, and a World War I couch. The kitchen area was sectioned off by a waist-high paneled divider. A small table with two chairs and the woodstove took up the entire floorspace of the kitchen. What really amazed me was the vast amount of cupboards she had. Floor-to-ceiling pantries lined three walls, with her sink positioned behind the living room divider. A natural spring provided the old woman's well with all the healthful mountain water she needed. At the far end of the living area was a curtained-off bathroom.

Obviously I was now sitting on No-Eyes' bed. The interior walls were a dingy brown-to-black, indicating a few ill-lit fires. Yet, as small as the cabin was and as sparsely as it was furnished, it had rapidly become a cozy second home to me. It was graciously appointed because of her presence.

As I was sitting there waiting for her to finish her breakfast, I suddenly became concerned if she had enough to eat. She certainly was forever full of child-like energy and she always appeared well and healthy. I returned my attention to the bare kitchen and took a disappointed note of its lack. It lacked any commercial food. My concern increased as I realized that she didn't even own a refrigerator. Then I logically reasoned that neighbors brought her food.

"Nope."

I was jarred out of my concentrated thoughts by a single syllable camouflaged by the muted munching of gums on cereal.

"Did you say something, No-Eyes?" I timidly asked, not being sure I had heard correctly.

"Yep."

Since the old woman didn't bother to reiterate what she had just said, I was left to mentally retrace what had transpired between us. After a quick review, I realized she had read my thoughts regarding the neighbors bringing food over for her. I silently considered her answer. If the neighbors don't bring in food and she doesn't ever go out for it, where does she get it?

Without breaking her calculated spoon-to-mouth meter, she replied, "Everywhere."

I was again confused. I threw in the towel and waited for her to place her empty bowl in the sink and join me in the living room.

She didn't. Instead she motioned for me to come into the kitchen. "No need market food. It bad for body."

"But No-Eyes, what do you eat?"

"Summer no think today! Summer's brain on strike?"

"What am I to think if nobody brings you food and you don't go out for any?"

"Who say I no go out for any, huh Summer, who?"

"You did!"

Here we go on another merry-go-round conversation again.

"Did not," she said sternly.

After retracing recent conversations, I came to the defeating conclusion that she was right, as usual.

"Alright, so you go out, but you certainly don't go to the market," I conceded.

"Blah!" was all she said as she turned to her eight-foot cupboard doors and banged each one open in turn. A veritable storehouse of edibles stared back at me as much as to say "see, stupid!"

I must have looked the stupid fool too, because I stood there, mouth gaping and feeling totally dumbfounded.

"Mountains my market," she proudly stated.

Behind the crude pantry doors were mason jars, rubber-stoppered vials, corked bottles, small and large boxes, tin containers and gallon jugs filled with all manner of seeds, pods, leaves and stems, flower petals, powders, nuts, and berries. She had enough stored away to feed all of the Fort Carson Infantry.

She grinned with justifiable satisfaction.

I was amazed. This needed closer inspection. I softly crept up to the packed shelves and read the heavily imprinted labels. Evidently she could read them like braille. I squinted as I tried to decipher her blind scribblings, and I discovered that she had everything grouped together in neat categories. I investigated further while she proudly stood by.

The grains were first. Large mason jars held pulverized seeds and roots. The labels read: Shepherd's Purse Flour, Sunflower, Sage, Cattail, Amaranth Meal, Lambs' Quarters Meal, and Purslane Meal.

"Makes tasty bread," she stated.

"These make bread?" I asked excitedly.

"You bet!"

I inspected the next grouping on her shelves. They were in a mixture of mason jars and boxes. This group seemed to be the largest. They were vegetables marked Milkweed Pods and Shoots, Wild Mushroom, Yampa Root, Wild Onion, Dandelion Green, Mesquite Green, Mountain Vetch Pea, Purslane Green, Amaranth Green, Plantain Green, Mountain Woodsorrel, Springbeauty Tuber, Indian Paintbrush Green, Elk Thistle Root, Miner's Lettuce, and Breadroot Tuber.

I was simply astounded at her wide variety of vegetables. She had more choices than I did in the largest supermarket, and I told her so. "This is amazing! I don't get this many vegetables in the market!"

Her grin was beaming with pleasure.

The next category seemed to consist of fruits and jams. I read with increasing interest, Rose Hip Jam, Squawberry Currants, Juniper Jam, Mountain Blueberry, Red-Fruited Gooseberry, Aromatic Wintergreen Jam, Wild Red Raspberry Jam, and Serviceberry Jam.

I anxiously followed the line of containers to small boxes containing spices of Wild Horseradish, Wild Mushroom, Onion and Mustard, Coltsfoot, Anise, and Wild Parsley.

The last group of foods consisted of a vast variety of tea makin's. Some were in powdered form in the rubber-stoppered jars, while others were already made up in the gallon jugs. There were Pine Needle Tea, Rose Hip Tea, Fireweed Tea, Dandelion Coffee, a Mesquite Drink, Spicebush Tea, Kinnikinnick Tea, Juniper Tea, Wintergreen Tea, Valerian Tea, Comfrey Powder, and Violet Leaf Powder.

Such was the incredible extent of the old woman's food supply. I cracked open one of the large jugs of tea and was nearly sent reeling back against her sink. The odor was pungent and horrid.

"That Valerian," No-Eyes giggled.

"That awful!" I teased back.

"Bad smell. Good bad-day medicine. Summer try."

"I'm having a fine day, thank you. I'll try it some other time." I quickly replied as I replaced the foul-smelling calmative back in its empty spot on her shelf.

No-Eyes shook her head. "Summer no judge by nose. Summer forget sticky lesson already."

The old woman was referring to a walk we had taken together the previous week. She was attempting to introduce me to the regional wildflowers while we gathered a massive bouquet for her table. I had spied a clump of tall, spiky flowers. Their purple blossoms were lovely and I thought their scent was unusually strong. I bent down and attempted to uproot several bunches in each hand.

No-Eyes slapped her bony knees in an uproarious laughter.

I didn't respond in kind as my hands came away from those beautiful flowers in a gooey, sticky mess.

"That Sticky Scorpion Weed. It weed!" she said through her crackling laughter as she held her nose between thin fingers. "It smell!"

"Thanks for the fair warning," I replied, trying to figure out what to do with the mess all over my hands. I knew she could differentiate every blade of greenery in that valley just through her acute sense of smell. She knew that I was about to grasp those purple stalks, but never made a move to forewarn me. Sometimes her lessons left me in a less-than-clean condition. This irritated me.

No-Eyes said I had just learned an important mountain lesson. I shouldn't judge anything by appearance, or smell, alone. She told me that if I had just paused a moment longer instead of instinctively grabbing, I would've seen all the ants stuck to the plant stems.

And that was the infamous "sticky" lesson she was referring to when I refused the Valerian Tea.

The old woman moved toward the last of three cupboards.

"See here, Summer."

I was flabbergasted to view the varied contents of the final cupboard. It was most likely more valuable than any other ingredients I'd reviewed up to this point. This cupboard contained tinctures and potions, liniments and ointments, poultices and pastes, oils, barks, powders, and extracts. This was her "big medicine" cabinet. It was a veritable pharmacy of concoctions. Again, bottles and jars were labeled Almond, Angelica, Arnica, Bilberry, Burdock, Chicory, Chickweed, Clover, Comfrey, Dock, Feverfew, Goldenrod, Goldenseal, Juniper, Mustard Seed, Myrrh, Oak Bark, Peppermint, Pine Needle, Puff Balls, Purslane, Sage, St. John's Wort, Shepherd's Purse, Stinging Nettle, Valerian, Wintergreen, Woodsorrel, Yarrow, and Yellow Dock.

"Cure all things," she informed me.

"Really?" I couldn't believe my eyes, or the statement.

No-Eyes perhaps read my doubt. She pulled a vial from the shelf and held it out for me to take. It was Peppermint Oil.

"Rub on man's back," she ordered.

She was telling me to use it on Bill's bad back. She was giving me a credibility lesson.

I sheepishly put it in my purse. Later I would massage it over his pinched nerve.

"When Summer convinced, she learn good medicine."

"I'd like that, No-Eyes. Do you really think I could? It must've taken a long time to know all you do about these herbs," I said, still looking over the enormous cabinet supply.

"What time? Time only in mind."

"Alright, I know. I can learn anything if I really want to."

She nodded slowly.

I noticed several unusually marked containers and I reached for one of them. The old woman slapped my hands. "You like baby near fire."

I immediately retracted my hand while she explained the last section of containers. They were not marked like the others were; however, she knew every one by its position and specific smell. The old one picked each one up and said what was in them. They were all deadly poisons.

"Baneberry, make heart stop. Death Camas, look like wild onion but worse than strychnine. Amanita, death mushroom. Poison Hemlock, very fatal. Lily of Valley, make heart stop and paralyze. Pasqueflower, make nerves depress. Bittersweet, stop heart. Buttercup, die of choking. Monkshood, paralyze lungs—die two hours. Columbine, have hydrocyanic acid—die of convulsions."

No-Eyes carefully replaced the last bottle back on its shelf. My mind was churning. Why does she need all of these horrible poisons? What on earth would an old woman do with fatal plants?

She slid her blind eyes up at me and gently closed the cabinet doors. "Medicine woman no good if not have complete supply."

That still didn't satisfy my mental question.

She knew that and explained that a modern-day pharmacy stocks every type of drug for every conceivable illness. Some of those drugs can be fatal if misused. A pharmacy even stocks poisons. The old woman gave viable examples of the occasional need to put a terminally ill animal out of its misery. There were many uses for the death poisons beside the killing of someone. She said my conditioned mind had created my unfounded suspicions. She was right, again.

The remainder of our day was spent in a rudimentary introductory course in the natural bounties of the mother earth. She demonstrated that she has generously provided man with everything he needs to eat well and to stay healthy. She said that most of the market food was harmful to the human systems. Beef and all red meats were number one on her list of forbidden foods. She said they are filled with a cancer. Lamb, fowl, fish, veal, or buffalo were alright if one really had to have animal meat. No-Eyes couldn't understand the need for killing animals when all of man's bodily nutrients could be simply derived from everything in her pantry. She said a handful of sunflower seeds contained more proteins than a steak. She expressed again and again that the Great Spirit gave us the fruit of the land for all our needs. She said the land is man's dining table and medicine chest.

When I had finished telling Bill about the old woman's food and medicinal supplies, he was quite impressed. We decided that it would be advantageous for me to learn all I could from her. I'm trying.

The Vision Quest

May your mind forever sparkle
like a star,
Your heart remain pure as
newfallen snow,
And your spirit forever sense
the wonderment of a child.

It was mid-summer. And for several weeks, my mind had been pestered by a particularly bothersome gnawing—as if you know you should be doing something but you don't know what it is. The uncomfortable intruder would be ever present within my daily thoughts. Sometimes it would charge darkly to the forefront of my mind. Most often, though, its menacing shadow would lurk behind the doors and around the corners of my mind.

It was the source of a constant irritation to me. Its unyielding persistence was a perturbing nuisance. I couldn't concentrate. I couldn't communicate with a clear-headed awareness without this unknown presence drawing my attention away. Something had to be done about it. Something had to transpire. I knew what that something was, and I had been hopelessly procrastinating.

For months now, I have been visiting No-Eyes. For months she has been teaching me the complex truths about the intricacies of life. I listened to her difficult discourses regarding the sacred flights of the spirit and I concentrated hard to gain the needed control in order to join her on these spirit wingings into other reality dimensions. I studied her herbal formulas. I accompanied her on countless, yet enjoyable, gathering expeditions where I learned the recognition and the practical medicinal or nutritional applications of each wild plant. I sat in silent respect as she revealed the identities and purpose of the Nature Spirits. Together we journeyed on the wind to distant worlds. She taught me to use my senses without the heaviness of the physical body limitations. With the patient help of No-Eyes, I reached out and touched the sun. Yet, with due respect to all I had learned, something was yet lacking. My spirit was restless. My mind was haunted with the specter of something yet undone.

I couldn't put my finger on this "thing" I had yet to do. I could not make a positive identification of it. This greatly upset me. I had finally reached the peak of my tolerance and made plans to take off for a couple of days in the mountains. I required total separation from everyone in order to deal with the force that was tailing me so relentlessly. I would have to draw it out in order to face it head on. I had my suspicions. I entertained the unpleasant idea that this persistent specter was my secret doubts, doubts regarding my future as revealed by No-Eyes. I didn't want a future like she so vividly pictured. I wanted to obliterate it with my own design. Paint it over with my own choice of pigments. I harbored, or created, a determination to make them untrue. The only way to settle these battling mental forces was to entirely disengage myself from the physical. I needed no people, no food, no interruptions. I needed positive proof of my purpose in life. I needed to stop relying on the words of No-Eyes and start seeking my own answers. I needed a vision quest.

Bill took off work for a couple of days in order to care for the girls. I kissed them all goodbye and left with only a knapsack on my back. I didn't need much, only a blanket or two for my bed, a small-caliber gun in case some wild creature took the notion that I'd make a tasty snack, and some miscellaneous items such as matches and first aid. They excitedly accompanied me to the edge of our meadow and watched me vanish into a mere speck on the mountainside.

I was entering the door of my first vision quest. I didn't know what to expect. I did know that I would stay until the specter of doubt had been vanquished from my mind. I wasn't afraid. Being with No-Eyes in all sorts of unknown situations and foreign surroundings banished my fears of the physical long ago. Knowing my family was in capable hands, I turned my full attention to the task at hand and began to let the Rocky Mountains do its thing on my senses. I became a living computer, taking in every minute piece of wondrous information around me. My physical intake was working overtime. I had to control the uptake or I would surely explode from sensory overload. I loved it.

Of course, my ultimate destination was our hidden valley. What more natural place for a quest of vision than sacred ground? I left the damp and warming meadow to enter a stand of Colorado Blue Spruce. The silvery-blue needles wavered up and down in the sweet breeze. They appeared to be nodding and whispering among themselves.

After a short time, I left the towering Christmas trees and set foot on the twisting path that would bear me through the crevice between mountains and into my land of yesterday. I advanced as far as I could before the first bend and I turned around to view our meadow far below me. Everything looked like small moving specks on a velvety carpet of green. Our neighbor had freed his horses and they were now romping about the harebells and yarrow. I couldn't see our cabin from my high vantage point, as it was sheltered behind one of the many hills of the valley. Nor could I hear the excited shouts and squeals from my girls who I knew were by now skinny-dipping in the cold waters of the stream. I murmured a loving farewell to our homey valley and rounded the bend toward a different kind of home.

The grade of the narrow ridge trail was quite steep. My legs were becoming tired and I was hungry. I had left the house without breakfast and my insides were boldly reminding me of that fact. I ignored their rumblings and centered my attention on the natural surroundings.

There was virtually no greenery growing along the ridge. Usually one sees trees sprouting miraculously out of the sloping rocks of the mountainside. Yet here, it was unusually barren. In a few scattered places, kinnikinnick creeped along a crevice; otherwise there was nothing but the dry and stoney soil. The jagged outcroppings of granite glimmered in the morning sunlight, shooting off sparkling rays of quartz and veins of pyrite. The trail itself was littered with the reflecting bits of mirror-like leaves of mica.

My legs ached and I was relieved to reach the pinnacle of my passageway. It would be all downhill from there on in, yet the walking wouldn't be much easier.

Finally the last bend was rounded and my heart drummed like a dozen tribes gathered in war ceremonies. The hidden sun had just cleared a billowing cloud and it flooded the valley in the brilliance of a thousand kleig lights. There was nothing mystical about it. It was sheer physical beauty. And I stood there becoming one with it.

My unity was sharply cut off by the slicing glide of the valley's resident peregrine falcon. With all conscious thought obscured, I observed the free-form flight of the magnificent bird. It gracefully weaved back and forth through the scented air of the valley. I experienced its weightlessness and felt the rushing breeze toss my hair behind me. I was in flight with the falcon and my spirit was free. I knew what it was like to hang in the sky, to feel the rush of air through flared

73

nostrils, to soar and dip and soar once again. The mountain peaks were easily skimmed and my breath taken away as the ground level fell suddenly away as we tilted and banked over vast expanses of lowlands. The falcon spied a furry prey. He zeroed in with incredible swiftness toward the dense forest.

The great bird had disappeared into the woods. I was left standing on the leading edge of the conifer forest in the valley. I had switched mental gears from observer to thinker. And I found myself not on the dry ridge road where I had first seen the falcon, but at meadow's edge down in the valley. I was there, all right. The swift-running stream was dancing fifty feet in front of me. I looked up at the ridge road where I had last held a conscious thought. I pondered the ramifications of my unconscious journey.

No-Eyes had made me believe that I'd done many unbelievable transportations. I had always held a thin thread of doubt about such mystical journeys. I attributed them to her amazing psychic talent. She had a way of getting into your head and leaving all sorts of impressions behind. I'm not one to be easily convinced just because I wanted it to be so. I was one who required proof. I was a skeptic of sorts. Yet, this present phenomenon baffled me entirely. One moment I was up on that ridge and the next moment I was down in the fertile valley. Of course, I realize I could've been so intensely engrossed in the falcon's flight, I could've been watching him all the while I was descending the trail. However, I don't recall watching where I was going. And that hazardous path required careful attention every step of the way. If I had looked down at my footings just once, my observation of the bird would've been completely broken off. I experienced no such break. His flight was one continuous journey. And the old Chippewa was nowhere around to place the happening in my head. Not this time.

I shook the bewildering experience from my mind and sorted out my equipment. I spent several hours carefully constructing my primitive, yet adequate, lean-to shelter. After surveying my work, and concluding that it was indeed satisfactory, I went to the stream for refreshment. The hunger pangs still persisted, yet not so boldly as before.

Being the only human in the valley, and knowing no other human could see me, gave me a sense of total aloneness. Not a lonesome kind of aloneness but a complete solitude. With this comforting solitude in mind, I shed my inhibitions and lay in the chilling whirlpool of the stream. I giggled at the sight of my clothing piled up among the wildflowers. Nowhere would I dare do a thing such as this except at my secret place in our own valley—and here. Usually there was always the possibility of someone seeing you; hikers, horse-riders, exploring tourists, wandering neighbors. I most certainly was not a nudist, and most certainly not an exhibitionist, yet the exhilaration derived from being in a natural and innocent surrounding, clothed only in the skin the Great Spirit gave you, gives one a rare opportunity to experience a real unity with nature.

The sun was set at high noon. The gentle breeze slowed to a baby's whimper. The perfumed air drifted in lazy waves about me and my body was totally relaxed in a natural whirlpool of cooling mountain waters. I knew I was becoming numb but I didn't care. I was completely relaxed and refreshed. I dug my toes deep into the shifting sands and watched the ripples reflect the sun's light in quivering mandalas over my body. The reflections twisted and changed as if looking into a child's multi-faceted kaleidoscope. It had a mesmerizing effect and I didn't want to be hypnotized while in the icy stream. I crawled out onto the soft meadow grass and stretched to the warming sun. Now I could easily recline in the tanning rays of the noonday warmth and nap a while.

The natural woodland sounds combined pleasingly with the constant rippling of the stream to create a perfectly harmonized lullaby. I quickly fell asleep in the protective arms of Mother Earth.

I immediately allowed my spirit to unfold its gossamer wings. I was in flight. I was free.

The landscape dropped away as I looked back at my restful body becoming smaller and smaller. I was at peace, both in the physical and in the spirit. I soared to the saw-toothed peaks of the mountains. I caught the updrafts and drifted effortlessly on the winds of time. I veered and fearlessly dove down into strange valleys. I paused in mid-air to hover over spectacular vistas. I thirstily drank of the bounty of nature's beauty. Her nectar was totally satisfying. My spirit encircled entire mountain ranges and it came to visit my own home valley. My three girls were still at our stream climbing over abandoned beaver dams, their favorite castles of fantasy. I left them and soared again, never wanting this incredible freedom to end. I was a falcon. I was pure spirit.

I shivered as a massive front of darkened clouds shrouded the warm sun and chilled my naked form. I awoke with a start and gathered up my clothes. Even though my dream was brought to an abrupt end, I took joy in its beauty and residual feeling of freedom. I was pleased to know my children were all right, and I now imagined them scurrying home in the face of an impending storm. They were mountain children, yet no child wants to be out in a threatening thunderstorm.

The lean-to was constructed to allow a fire at the meadow's edge to reflect on the branches behind me. I didn't bother with a fire yet, as it was only late afternoon and even though the cloud cover was heavy, it was still mildly warm in the valley. I hated wasting good wood. Perhaps at dusk I would light the fire.

The spirits of nature were having a mischievous time showing off. The clouds became darkly ominous and tumbled over and over each other in a vain attempt to gain recognition as leader of the nimbus pack of ruffians. Thor bellowed and echoed his booming authority back and forth between the darkened ranges. The wind cracked its forceful whip over the bent backs of the subjugated aspens and willows. The sky changed its ominous robe from a dusty gray to a menacing and billowing cloak of ebony. Nature was showing its dark side, and it was magnificent in its stark raving beauty.

I observed it.

I felt the intense power in the blinding lightning that etched its signature across the blackboard sky. My entire body reverberated with each resounding boom of thunder and I raced and swirled with the wind as it tore over everything in its way. I was experiencing unbelievable power. I was feeling deadly forces. I was the dark side of nature. Yet, with this force and power, I sensed an inner core of calm, a love.

The seemingly malevolent force turned out to be nothing but a threat. The wild wind bore the blackened clouds over some other mountain range and left my valley in its wake of peace. It was quickly bathed in the natural light of dusk. I made my fire.

The erratic flames danced wildly about as they licked at the blackness around them. I loosely wrapped a woolen blanket about my shoulders and watched the fire's dervish performance. I didn't actually require a roaring fire for warmth as the summer night was mild and the heavens were clear, brightened by a friendly full moon.

The night was alive with a thriving nocturnal population. If you listened hard you could hear a virtual pandemonium of tongues. The separate languages were as individual and distinct as the native speech of foreign nations. The pine marten chattered wildly from a distant tree. Somewhere far up on the mountainside a cougar screamed its victory over an unwary prey. A lone howl signaled methodically to a separated pack of coyotes. The thick underbrush rustled with the passing of a pair of striped skunks. The horned owl hooted humorously from somewhere deep in the conifer woods behind me. Various chitterings and chatterings gave warnings of a stranger in their midst. Branches bobbed with the restlessness of squirrels. And farther downstream, loud splashes could be detected from the massive tails of the industrious beavers. Birds, too, were sounding their intermittent evening calls. The scampering and rustling, the seeking and hiding of the hunter and the hunted would continue well until dawn.

I curled down in my wool blanket and stared up into the vibrant night sky. The night heavens are the original timepiece of God. I looked into the crystal face of that timepiece and could well visualize the invisible workings behind it. Greatness created the well-oiled gears that ever so slowly turned the brilliant cogs of man's time. Its massive scope carefully moves about millions of points of reference to precisely calibrated junctures. I can almost hear the audible clink as each constellation ticks into its respective position. If you bother to watch, you'll actually see its minute rotation. Watching the grand timepiece move must be similar to the astronauts viewing the slow rotation of the earth from deep space. Indeed, it is one and the same. I was totally immersed in the vastness of it all.

Suddenly my spine tingled and the hair on the back of my neck prickled. Something was not right. Something was very wrong. I sensed the familiar warnings of an uninvited presence. My first thought was to reach for the gun at my side. However, a mere physical weapon is powerless against a psychic force. I remained frozen in position and drew on my mental resources. My defenses were already strongly in place when I noticed an unusual faint brightness to my right. It came from the general direction of the woods.

I knew I had to face whatever was there. It didn't appear to be advancing toward me. It just remained stationary, watching. Moisture seeped through my pores. And I slowly turned my head to face the source of the unknown force.

I jumped.

A man stood at the forest edge. A man clothed in light. He stood motionless with one hand raised, two fingers extended up. I took this as a friendly sign of peace and shakily I acknowledged the greeting with a like gesture. My sweating subsided and the stiff hairs relaxed. However, I was still experiencing the uncomfortable tingling of my spine.

"May I warm myself by your fire?" came a mellow voice.

He didn't look as though he needed any warming and I hesitated, still extremely wary.

"I'll not harm you," he reassured.

I wasn't exactly reassured either.

"All right then, I'll just sit here." He sat cross-legged on the leaves and forest debris. His smile touched my heart with warmth.

We sat staring at one another for several minutes. I knew he was telepathically sending me messages. I was receiving definite feelings of incredible love, unbelievable intelligence, and greatness. I gathered my calmed wits and found my shaky voice.

"You may join me if you wish," I offered feebly.

In an effort to reinforce my confidence, he remained seated.

"I can feel the warmth from here, thank you."

"Who are you? Where did you come from? I thought I was the only one in this valley," I asked warily. I was deeply mortified to think back on my uninhibited venture in the stream earlier that day. How dare anyone invade my private sacred ground?

He calmly responded to my fearful questions in a systematic fashion.

"I am a completed one. I come from everywhere and no, you are never alone, anywhere."

This was like talking with No-Eyes. I was getting answers that only provoked more questions. Answers that were no answers. Realizing this being wasn't going to cause me any physical or psychic harm, I let out my usual sigh. It served to relax me and my computer began calculating in a logical fashion. I reran the skimpy conversation so far and analyzed it.

"You're an enlightened being," I tested.

He nodded.

"You can be anywhere."

Again an affirmative motion.

"And I already know I'm never really entirely alone."

"Good," he whispered.

"Are you my vision?"

"That is for you alone to decide," he calmly stated.

Oh, great, this was like talking to a psychologist. Questions were always answered with other questions. I continued to try to find the lead string to this present ball of tangled verbal yarn.

"Why are you here?"

"Why do you think I'm here?"

"To teach me something."

He again nodded.

"To teach me something No-Eyes can't...."

He shook his head.

"Does No-Eyes know what you're going to say?"

He nodded again.

"Then why didn't *she* tell me?"

He got up and moved closer to the fire. He was sitting directly in its light, yet he didn't appear any brighter. His own aura outshone the firelight.

"Think."

I thought. I didn't want to admit my reason for coming here on my vision quest. I didn't want to verbalize the stinging doubts that I was ashamed of. Then I reasoned that if he was who I thought he was, he could surely read me loud and too clear. I knew it would be of no practical use to hide anything from this man.

"Because I would doubt her words."

"Precisely," he affirmed.

"Do I have justifiable cause for such doubt?"

"That is for you to decide."

"But how? I want to believe everything she said. And I did, until she began talking about my future. I'm only an ordinary person."

The man reached his hand out to me.

"Take my hand. Let me show you something."

I took his warm hand and we were instantly in another forest. I felt rather like old Scrooge in the power of Marley. I could tell that this forest was somewhere near timberline because of the masses of slender engelmann spruce growing profusely about. To our right was a huge white marble monument of some sort. It stood maybe ten feet high and was rectangular in shape. It was a thick, heavy marker.

"Read it," he coaxed.

I looked at him and left his side to give the giant stone closer inspection. I traced the deeply engraved lettering with my fingers. The White Brotherhood. The name was vaguely familiar. No-Eyes had mentioned it only once during our many conversations. She never expanded on it and I never had the presence of mind to question her further. I turned back to the man.

"What does it mean?" I queried.

"Come, let us walk a ways, my friend."

He motioned for me to walk at his side, yet he never touched me. I had the distinct feeling I wasn't supposed to have physical contact with him unless he initiated it.

"The White Brotherhood is an organization of spirits. These being both in the etheric and physical realities. Follow me?"

It was now my turn to do the nodding.

"This organization was formed to aid God in the restoration of floundering souls. Mind you, my friend, God needs no aides; however, we *want* to help in retrieving His spirits back to Him. The organization is comprised of completed spirits who have chosen to remain in order to guide and instruct. Some of these willingly return to physical forms and bring to the world great knowledge and enlightenment. They have vital physical missions. Other members are near completion and wish to finish their circle of return by aiding those on earth. These also serve as guides and helpers. Then there are those enlightened spirits who occupy physical human bodies to bring the truth of reality to the masses. All these comprise The White Brotherhood. As you can see, my friend, it is an unusual organization. It is of the highest and purest form of intelligence."

I thought over all I had heard.

"What does this Brotherhood have to do with me, though?"

"Did I say that it had anything to do with you?"

"No."

"Did anyone?"

"No."

"Did anyone ever?"

"No," I replied too hastily. No-Eyes had previously mentioned a Mountain Brotherhood comprised of local mountain people who were aware of certain truths. That light bulb was flashing in my brain, and I was virtually shocked at the inferred implications. He broke my reverie.

"Well, then, perhaps you are correct," he replied as he gently touched my hand.

The dawn's light made me squint as it slipped its long arm over the far ridge. I turned my head to avoid its pointing finger. It was morning and I was hungry and confused. The birds created a riotous commotion as I tried to sort out the night's events. I remembered being fascinated by the stars and planets of the night sky. I remembered the sudden entry of an unknown force that interrupted that fascination. At that precise point, I must've fallen asleep and the man was simply a figment of my dream world. I had dreamt the man, our journey, The White Brotherhood, and all of it. And I was hungry.

My campfire was out, yet, out of habit I kicked some dirt in it just to make sure. As I trekked around the burnt leftovers, I noticed a flattened section of the meadow grass. It was next to the campfire, precisely where the man in my dream would've sat. I took several steps backward toward the forest and came across another flattened area. My heart lunged.

"Nah, couldn't be," I rationalized, "couldn't be."

Since I had no breakfast to prepare, I headed directly toward the stream for an early-morning bath. The day was hinting at a perfect specimen of a mountain summer. The obvious signs were all there, even the more obscure ones. It was going to be clear and exceptionally warm. I was going to ignore my hunger by observing the beauty of my secret valley. I was determined that my mind would emerge the triumphant victor over the physical wants of my body. The routine gnawing was a conditioned reaction that the mind could regulate at will. The mind need not be enslaved by the childish rantings of the physical. It needed a simple adjustment in programming. I was about to accomplish this by first ignoring my stomach's inconsiderate tantrums.

The grassy edge of the stream was still damp with dew. My feet dangled in the coursing waters as I lay back on the wet grass to watch the drifting clouds come and go at their leisure. It was an amusing child's game. I tried to make out different shapes from the ever-changing cloud formations. It was a pastime reserved for those who were rich with time. I had all the time in the world. A horse wafted by and quickly changed into a scotty dog. The transformations rolled by in a lazy procession of mutating characters. A mass of nothingness entered my scope of vision.

I watched it.

Nothing.

I waited for a formation to build.

Nothing. It wasn't even moving any more. The winds must've died down considerably. Suddenly a huge rectangular shape rose up from the mass of barely rolling cloud. I was no longer watching with childish intent. I was observing.

I was as light as air, lighter than air. The center of the misty nebula was a foundation for the great marker that rose up from its base. I touched it. A transparent door opened inward and I entered.

I stood there for a long while watching what was going on inside. The vast room could easily have housed the entire Pentagon building. I had never seen such an enormous enclosed area. It must've been large enough to shelter a dozen football fields. Yet, the size was only a small aspect of my amazement. What was equally astonishing was the masses of people inside. It was virtually a buzzing metropolis.

The massive interior was circular. Hundreds of large rooms connected one after another all the way around it. The walls were constructed of a brilliant white material with minute specks of sparkles entwined in it. It was cool to the touch. Above each door was a sign indicating what that specific room was used for. Some signs I readily understood, some I didn't. In the center of this vastness was a glass podium with a mammoth book on it. Beside the book was a complex network of computers.

My footfalls were silent as I curiously moved from room to room. A door was ajar. I peered through its narrow opening.

"Curiosity killed the cat!" someone whispered behind me.

If I'd had a body to contend with, I know I would've jumped a mile. I swung around to see my visitor with the body of light. This time he was garbed in a long, white hooded robe. His bright aura could not be concealed, however.

"Shouldn't I be here?" I questioned softly.

He chuckled and extended his arm out toward the core of the room. "Nobody gets in here unless they're meant to."

I grinned back at him.

"Why was I meant to?"

"We'll get to that in time, my friend. First you must thoroughly understand where you are, then we can get down to personal matters."

We walked, or glided, to the great book. He opened it up and pointed, indicating that I should read what was there. I looked at him with hesitation.

"Go ahead, it's perfectly all right."

I furtively glanced about the room to see if anyone was watching me. Nobody was. They were all deeply engrossed in their own business. I followed his finger down an encyclopedic list of names. The movement stopped and so did my heart. There in that massive book, in the middle of who knows where, were my two names.

"What does this mean? Why are my names in this book?"

"That's an excellent place to begin. Do you have any idea where you are?"

"The other side?" I answered timidly.

"Sort of. You see, my friend, the 'other side' is simply a different dimension of reality. Look about you. All these people here are spirits. This is where everyone's spirit comes between physical lifetimes. The door you entered through is only for those spirits seeking the truth. The spirits of those who have died enter by quite another door. There, they are met by their personal guide and the spirits of their formerly deceased relatives and friends. Those relatives and friends help the newly crossed-over spirit adjust to its new surroundings. It is their job to re-acquaint the newly arrived spirit with its old domain. In essence, this is a processing point for arrivals and departures. Depending on what the newly arrived spirit requires for its advancement to God, we have extensive accommodations to meet all their needs."

He patted the book.

"This book is called The Book of Records. In it are the physical life recordings of every spirit's life. It is a Book of Balances by which we can determine at a glance what an individual spirit needs to correct in order to bring itself into a more perfect state. Every infraction of God's Law is recorded here. Every good deed and thought is also recorded. These are precisely weighed to determine if another physical lifetime will be required of that spirit."

"What does mine say?"

He closed the book with a reverberating thud.

"We'll get to that, my friend."

He showed me the computer.

"This is used to classify and narrow down one's chosen future lifetime. For an example, let's say that after a newly arrived spirit has duly rested and studied his personal record of accounts, he is now prepared to return for another physical lifetime. He carefully calculates those faults he needs to balance out. Perhaps he had been bestowed with riches in his last life, yet he greedily hoarded those riches and didn't share them with those less fortunate. This next lifetime will have to have that selfishness entirely balanced out. Perhaps he wishes to be reborn to poor parents and spend the rest of his new lifetime in poverty. Or he has many other options, such as becoming a missionary or a physician in a poverty-stricken land. In this manner, he is balancing out his former selfishness by a new lifetime of total unselfish giving of himself.

"This computer seeks out his needed requirements for such a life and narrows down the biological parental possibilities. From these, he chooses who his parents will be in his new life."

It was all thoroughly logical to me; however, I had a few questions I needed answers to.

"This is logical to me, but what of the fact that the spirit's memory of all this is not retained? How does a person remember why he is even alive? And what if he strays from his intended purpose?"

"Slow down, my friend. One question at a time. First of all, every time a spirit comes back here he spends a great deal of time planning and studying God's truths. In a like manner, every time a spirit returns to the physical, he is a little bit more aware of those truths. He may not noticeably remember them, but at least there will be the impetus to question and seek them out. This also relates to your second question. An aware individual inherently knows he is alive for some specific purpose. Usually the paths he chooses lead him to his goal, or at least close enough to it. Thirdly, many do stray from their intended purpose. God gave each spirit a great gift when He created them. He gave them a free will. Many times that very gift is the cause of a spirit wasting an entire lifetime, only causing him to return to try once again. For nobody returns to God until they have been reborn, again and again. This is the law. It is fair."

I thanked him for clarifying my questions, but I had many more.

"How does the spirit enter a physical body?"

He smiled.

"Those things are not important here. No-Eyes can answer those for you. I have more to show you; come."

We left the center of the room and I followed his lead. We arrived at the first of the many doors. It was marked: Comfort.

"This is where newly arrived spirits spend much time dealing with the separation from loved ones left behind in the physical. Most new spirits have no more earthly concerns; however, there are those who need this sort of way station."

He silently cracked the door open to reveal a huge room where loving spirits were comforting grieving ones. The grieving souls were shown how well the ones left behind would get along. They eventually realized that the physical grief was a needed way to deal with life and it served as a strengthener.

My guide opened the next door marked: Love. These spirits were virtually melting into other spirits in order to share a profound and pure love.

"Life in the physical can be a heavy burden which leaves ugly scars upon the spirit. Oftentimes, an individual's life was miserably lived in a vacuum. This vacuum had no inward or outward expressions of affection, caring, or love. Consequently, exceedingly lonely spirits cross over and they are in a desperate need of that affection which it so pitifully lacked in its physical life."

He led me to the next door labeled: Peace. Inside, these spirits were basking in a lush pastoral setting. It reminded me of my hidden valley.

"Each spirit is reborn in order to balance out a negative. Therefore, most lives are spent in a race against time. Some lives are hectic and harrowing. Here, they regain that required inner peace their restless physical bodies never gave them."

We continued past several dozen more doors. He explained that beyond each door, spirits were revitalizing their needs. One couldn't be reborn unless the spirit itself was perfectly balanced in its emotional and personality requirements.

At the end of the wide circle of rooms was a door that was not marked. We paused near it, yet not too close.

"And what is this room for?" I asked of my guide as I made an advancing movement.

"No, my friend, we will not crack that one open."

I gave him a quizzical look and backed away.

"Beyond that door is what those yet in the physical call Hell."

I backed closer to his side.

"Do not be afraid. Did I not say that this was the 'other side?' I meant it to include *all* sides."

"But I thought you also said this is an arrival and departure station. How can those in there depart?"

"They chose to depart from God. They rebelled in their lifetimes time after time. They refused to acknowledge God as their ultimate goal. They chose their easy path of evil over the difficult path to God."

"What is it like in there?"

"Nothing. It is a great nothing for all eternity."

I didn't know what to say. I felt such a heaviness for those poor lost souls.

"Come, let me show you something that may cheer you."

I followed the man in white to a door that we had passed over. It was labeled: Mercy.

"I will not open this one either. Yet I want you to know how understanding God is. Beyond this door are all the spirits who lived their physical lives as religious skeptics and confirmed atheists. They committed one of the most grave mistakes while on earth. They denounced a living God. They believed in no afterlife. Yet, here they are in this room being shown God's bountiful mercy. They exist in a glow of God's love. They will never doubt again.

"You see, my friend, God has an endless supply of rope which He continually lets out. God never condemns anyone. They hang themselves. However, one such grave infraction does not condemn a spirit. God takes them back and loves them. After their spirits are filled to capacity, they will never again question the existence of a supreme being."

"Is there a limbo here? A place where non-Christian babies go?" I asked, looking for a likely door.

He laughed a resounding roar.

"Were you listening at all? Would God banish from Himself spirits that only existed in an infant form? Those spirits had no free will to choose! No, my friend, spirits of dead unbaptized infants merely return here like all the others. You'd do well to remember that baptism is an affair of the individual's spirit, not a contrived religion. All religions are comprised of God's spirits. All people are alive merely because of the simple fact that God's spirit dwells within their physical form. Specific sect beliefs have no bearing on the reality you see before you here.

They all end up here, no matter what they believe.

"Also, I might remind you that everyone's spirit was created in the first days of creation. How could God condemn an old spirit to such a place as limbo when that very same spirit is eons old? Think about that."

"Then there is no purgatory either," I concluded.

"The physical *is* purgatory. The physical is the ground level where spirits have the golden opportunity to balance out their wrongdoings, pay for former disobedience of God's Laws, make themselves better."

He didn't give me any time to digest all the things he had shown me and talked about. He turned with a flurry of his long robe and strode across the vast expanse of the great hall. He stood in front of The Book of Records and called me over to join him.

"Now, what were you asking about this book?"

"I wanted to know what it said about me."

He peered down at me beneath his furrowed brows.

"Are you absolutely sure you want to know?"

I hesitated, then nodded.

"Well, look for yourself then. It's all there." He held out his palm in an inviting gesture.

I approached the Book. My heart was throbbing wildly as I read my record of lifetimes. On the bottom line was my present intended purpose for this one.

My legs were numb from the cold stream waters. I could barely lift them out onto the dry grass. The sun was past its noonday position. I had obviously slept a long time. Vigorous rubbing quickly restored the healthy tone of my legs, and I stamped around to make sure they were in peak working order.

The sun was blinding as I peered through my shielding fingers for the cloud of my dream. The sky was filled with an opaque turquoise liquid. It was unmarked by any imperfections of white wispy material. I returned my gaze to the pristine valley and saw it in a new light. It would always be my sacred ground, the place that gave me my vision. Yet something was different about it now. I couldn't get a fix on what I was sensing.

I walked the entire length of the stream. The willows were alive with vibrant life. The wildflowers offered up their sweet gifts to me as I passed by. The stream repeated its message over and over as I accompanied it on its endless journey. I picked a golden banner and held it tenderly in my hand. Its velvety pocketed petals reflected the sunlight and gave it a living glow. It had contained the force of life. At that moment it was the most beautiful thing I'd ever seen. The entire meadow was a shimmering testimony of God's love for me and my fellowmen. I was a witness to the magnificent splendor of the Great Spirit's creations in nature. I had observed this nature and become one with it. I had unfolded the delicate wings of my spirit and soared in the majestic flight with the falcon. And in so doing, I became one with All That Is.

Even though my quest was completed, I remained that night to contemplate in the solitude of my sacred ground. I stared up into the grand timepiece and saw the hand of God behind it. I peacefully watched the glowing embers of my fire and I listened to the friendly sounds of the deep forest. I was basking in a contentment little known to man. I knew why I was here.

The following morning I awoke before daybreak. I gathered up my belongings and crossed the damp meadow in the predawn light. The trek up the ridge was not so strenuous, even though I had had nothing to eat for two days. The high point of the trail came quicker than I had anticipated. Once I rounded that bend, the valley would be but a treasured memory. I paused to take in its loveliness for the last time. It still appeared entirely different to me.

In the semidarkness, it was silently shrouded under a rolling mist. Faint chirpings were just now beginning. My land was still drowsy with sleep. I strained to hear the stream's farewell message. As I stood listening, a golden ray shot over the eastern ridge and speared the heart of the mist. And as I viewed the rich masterpiece below me, I realized why my valley looked different. It hadn't changed at all. I had.

Into Hades— A Journey

*May you ever hold hands with Faith,
And may the Great Spirit be your
eternal Beacon.*

A dark mood shrouded Woodland Park. Once again it was blanketed with the thick fog that occasionally settles in between the mountain ranges. The mid-summer day was reduced to the light of a gray London evening. Bill and I had planned to picnic with our girls. Obviously, this wasn't the perfect day for such a gay activity. We were forced to be homebound. So instead, we played games of Life, Monopoly, and half a dozen card games. Finally we were played out. Even the girls were weary.

We sat around the living room floor and began discussing spiritual concepts. Aimee started it out by inquiring why God condemned his own spirits to a hell. These out-of-the-blue questions always led to lengthy explanations. I had written a children's picturebook entitled: *Mountains, Meadows and Moonbeams.* This book explained all the spiritual concepts I learned from entities such as No-Eyes. I illustrated each concept in order to clarify meanings for the child. As yet, this book has not been published, so don't look for it. However, I use it to aid my own children with their understanding. Aimee's question prompted me to bring the book back out and reexplain our purpose here, why every person is here.

No-Eyes had her own way of explaining that often-asked question. Although I never asked her about hell, she took it upon herself to introduce me to it. From previous discussions Bill and I had with another entity, we already knew about the subject. I suppose No-Eyes felt I needed an explicit elaboration. At any rate, I will share it now.

One summer day, when the flood of tourists was bloating the highways to near bursting, I ventured out to No-Eyes' place. As usual, it was a perfect mountain morning. After we finished our Rite of Thanksgiving and Greeting, we remained inside her cool cabin. We talked lightly of general topics while we shared one of her unique tea blends. It would appear that there was no outlined lesson plan for this day. I was to find out how wrong I was. It was comforting to be able to enjoy the old woman's casual talk. We were as friends visiting one another. There was no mention, or even a hint, of special instruction. Until she suddenly ordered me to sit on the couch while she pulled over her trusty rocker. I should have known. The woman never wasted a day that could be spent teaching a valuable lesson, lessons that profit the spirit.

"Summer sit on couch now."

I did.

"Summer gonna go somewheres."

"You coming too?"

"Nope."

"Why not?"

"No-Eyes already been. Summer's turn."

"Can't we both go?"

"I no want to go again. No-Eyes not ever gonna go again."

Oh, great! Now where was she sending me? I had learned to go alone to different places while she accompanied me in her mind (observation, remember?).

I had the awful sinking feeling that I was going to be exposed to negative forces again. The old one had taken me to various groups that were dabbling in dark forces. She had successfully brought me through them, carefully watched my reflexes, reactions, and responses, and then safely brought me back. She had told me at that time that one day I would have to go to the ultimate center of evil. She also was honest enough to inform me that I would be going alone—but not before she was certain I was ready to handle it. My butterflies confirmed my dreaded thought that today was that day of days. I shook with a sudden nervous spasm.

"Summer cold?"

"You know I'm not."

"Summer scared, huh."

"Of course I'm scared."

"Summer be okay."

90

"That's easy for *you* to say, you're staying here."

"I be there, up here." She nodded her head.

"That's not the same and you know it."

"What so! Just as long as Summer know it."

That comment really made me nervous. I knew that if she was psychically with me she could observe *only*. I needed her there *actually* (spirit body) so she could help me if I needed it. She was no help just being there psychically. I was really scared.

"Summer put up protection now."

I worked. I worked harder than I had ever worked in my life. This could very well cost me my life. This was no beaver pond. This *was* life. It was *real*.

"Not good enough!"

I reinforced my visualization. The psychic shield glowed and quivered with an undulating whiteness. It was good.

"No good! Need *more!*"

I gave it all the strength my energy dynamo could generate.

"Nope!"

I visualized God. We held hands. The shield was shimmering with a blinding forcefield.

"Whew! Now that *something*! We gonna go now. Summer ready?"

I nodded. I never could speak from here on in, as that could very possibly cause a break in the protection. Of course, seeing Whose image I had borrowed, I rather doubt any such break was possible. Still, I wasn't taking any foolish chances. Would you?

No-Eyes was mentally creating my etheric path. She worked in silence. Oftentimes, when she went with me in this manner, she would precede me by forming a sort of road by which my spirit followed to its final destination. She did this now as I anxiously waited. I firmly held onto the mystical hand. I was squeezing the energy essence from it—probably hoping the powerful essence would infiltrate my own weak one.

"I done," she whispered.

I heaved in a deep breath and let it slowly exhale. I calmed my senses, all the while never losing sight of my powerful protective vision. This took incredible concentration. From here on in I would have to see whatever it was I was supposed to see, all the while *never* losing sight or strength of my protective shield. I would have to hold two thoughts, see two things simultaneously. If I lost sight or thought of my protection for a fraction of a second, it could be a fatal mistake. I would expose the spirit to a shock (evil attack) which would then follow the etheric lifeline back to the physical body where the wave would then trigger a massive heart attack or worse (possession). I knew what the stakes were. They were the highest they'd ever get. If No-Eyes thought I was ready, I took confidence in that judgment.

I left. I hovered above the restful physical form and I energized my shield. I looked around me and saw the old one concentrating. I could tell she was terribly anxious—the first time I had seen her so anxious that she sat poised on the edge of her chair.

I left the cabin and, directly in front of me, was her strong trail. It gleamed with her energy. I followed, never taking my eyes from it. One minute I was in the third dimension and the next minute I wasn't. Nothing in my peripheral vision was familiar. Yet, never did I take my eyes from the old woman's path. I could feel her constant reinforcement. I squeezed the hand.

An unidentifiable sound came to my awareness, a mumbled sound of many voices. I continued on the glowing trail, never veering from it.

A deafening laughter entered my ears. Gurgles were intertwined with agonizing screams. I remembered my "listening lesson" and I let the sounds run through my head without giving the actual awareness of listening. I never could actually perform the conscious act of listening. Wavering forms wove around me. I kept my eyes on the woman's path. Enormous snakes slithered around my feet. They opened jaws that exposed fangs dripping with slime. They altered forms and turned into Medusa-like creatures that slobbered in my face. I squeezed and squeezed that powerful hand.

Terrifying, stinking and deformed humans spat in my eyes. They gibbered and gesticulated obscenely about me in a grotesque dance of the doomed.

I knew I was terrified, yet I dare not ever think it. The path continued.

The initial muted sounds turned into wails and cries as I neared my destination. The shimmering path was becoming shorter. I could now see when it ended. I thought of the forceful shield. I thought how beautiful and good it was amidst the vileness around it. "God and beautiful. God of power and light. God of power and light. God most powerful. God most powerful."

My progress was slower. "God most powerful."

Putrid smells.

"God most powerful. Goodness. Strength of light."

The glorious trail amid the stench of rotting beings ended. My path was *gone!*

"Light of God! *Light of powers! Goodness of God!*" I squeezed the hand. The hand was *gone!*

Vile words. Spit. Rancid breath. Closing in.

I desperately reached out within my shield. I frantically visualized another entity. I squeezed.

It squeezed back.

"Powers of light! Powers of light! Power of powers!"

Silence. Void. Blackness.

I stood, maintaining my shield vision. I well knew what my friend looked like—my friend who belonged to the replacement hand. We were still together. We had survived.

A brilliant pinpoint of brightness pierced the blackness that surrounded us.

I watched in fascination.

It enlarged.

My hand was being pulled down. I looked to my friend. He was kneeling. I immediately followed his example. Could this be? Could this be what I was thinking? No. Yet my friend, my right-handed entity, was kneeling in total reverence with bowed head. I too looked down into the void.

The total blackness brightened. It began to shimmer. It wavered. I closed my eyes. I was more frightened than ever. The blinding light penetrated my eyelids and I was filled with a great warmth. It flooded my being and that of my dear friend. I cried.

The light remained ever so momentarily. Then it began to lessen.

I felt my friend pull me up.

I dared to open my eyes.

The pinpoint was just vanishing into the void.

We looked at one another.

He smiled compassionately. "We will speak of this when I next come. Peace, Mary."

I was alone. I thought of the cabin.

No-Eyes whispered to me. "That too close. Good thing Summer think so fast of him."

Silence. I was in a beautiful state of memory. I never wanted to speak again. I closed my eyes and lay on the soft cushions of the worn couch.

No-Eyes knew. She busied herself in her kitchen while I reveled in my residual effects of bliss. I think I fell asleep, for when I awoke, the slanting rays of the sun were long and orange.

"Summer okay?"

"Yes."

"Summer have close call."

"Yeah."

"Want to go home now?"

"Not yet. I need to talk about it."

"Okay. Here, drink this."

I took the steaming brew of herbs. I was deeply contemplative; not really wanting to talk, yet I had to.

"What Summer want to know?"

There was so much. "Well, my protective visualization worked real good up to a point. And when I needed it the most, it was gone."

"Summer pick bad power to be with."

"*Bad*! I picked God's own likeness!"

"Calm down. Think. Where trail lead?"

"Hell. You made me a trail straight into hell."

"What hell, Summer?"

The bare fact dawned brightly in my mind. "Of course! I used God's hand to hold onto and hell is the *absence* of God!"

She grinned with my sudden realization.

I didn't grin. "You knew He would leave my side, didn't you."

She nodded rather guiltily.

"Then why didn't you say so when I formed it within my shield? Why didn't you tell me to pick another?"

"I no could choose for you."

"That's why you were so nervous and anxious, wasn't it?"

Another affirmative nod.

I thought on that. She wouldn't be always at my side to catch the spilt milk. I needed to be on my own, as I soon would be.

"Summer angry at No-Eyes?"

I held her rough hand. "No. You do what you have to do."

"Summer do what Summer have to do too. Summer bring him in fast."

"I thought of him right away. He's brought us through a lot."

"I know."

I sat back and smiled. I hesitated.

"Say it, Summer."

Tears were forming.

"It okay." She moved next to me on the couch and put her thin arm around me.

I leaned into her breast and let her hug tight while I cried.

"That natural. It okay."

I couldn't control the sobbing. It was relief and awe all at one time.

94

"I was so *scared*! I was trying so hard. I almost lost sight of the shield a couple of times. I was so scared. Those things were awful. Then, when the hand was gone I was terrified! Then I thought of Bill's guide and everything changed." I wiped my red eyes, looked up at No-Eyes, and said a stupid thing. "Hell is hell."

She grinned. "That right."

I laughed.

"That what hell be alright."

"No-Eyes?"

"What?"

"He was so beautiful."

"He that alright."

"My friend seemed to feel at home with Him."

"Yep."

"Why does he bother with us when he could be with God?"

"That his job. Summer already know that."

"Yeah, I suppose, still . . ."

"No still. All spirits have special jobs."

"The light was like nothing I could ever compare it to."

"It *have* no stuff to compare to. *No* stuff like *that* light!"

"I guess so." I was in that mood again. Words sounded so insignificant.

"Summer go home now. Summer feel better."

"No-Eyes, if only people could see hell."

"Yep."

"If only they could see . . . ."

"Summer go now."

The drive home that glorious night was slow and mesmerizing. I had to digest all I had been through that day. Hell, then Heaven, all in one day was too much for a simple human mind to sufficiently grasp. The vile stench of hell was unforgettable. The agonizing suffering was incomprehensible. My thoughts turned to the brilliant pinpoint of light that grew to an unfathomable size of blinding essence. I would never forget how the tender warmth of love permeated every etheric cell of my spirit.

Later, much later, the horrors of Hades faded from my memory. They were sympathetically replaced with the memory of a sparkling light. The light shone constantly within my simple being. The light would forever after lessen my daily troubles. The light gave me acceptance. It gave me a deep, deep love and understanding. In my world of skeptics and the unaware, the light was to be my eternal beacon.

Flight of the Spirit

*May you always unfold your night
wings wide,
And treasure the visions
of the dreamer.*

I was having the time of my life excitedly weaving in and out of the colorful shops of San Francisco. Each import place was so entirely different and unique from the next. Bill was engrossed in a store across the street. I entered an oriental shop and as I reached the shelf overflowing with miniature Buddhas, the figurines shook ever so slightly. Nobody else noticed the faint movement. I trembled with the possible implications of my lone observation. I glanced around at the other customers. They were chatting and obviously unconcerned.

Suddenly a deafening groan echoed through the shop as the floor uplifted and lowered in a wave from one end to the other. The large picture window blew out. Glass was flying and shattering about everywhere. Shelves fell to the floor. People screamed and dashed wildly about. Great cracks rent the walls. The ceiling began to crash down in massive chunks. The groan increased in intensity and was accompanied by a great tearing sound.

I ran shakily out of what was left of the old building. Devastation was rampant everywhere I looked. Buildings were hollowed out. Bricks and debris filled the air, flying in all directions. Water was swiftly oozing up from the enormous crack in the street. The crack grew with amazing speed.

Bill was on the other side. He tried to get to me. The ground was shaking so bad he was on his hands and knees. He kept falling over on his side.

The crack grew wider. The ground creaked and groaned. It was deafening. Finally the crack split the street in two. It ran up the street, through the city, and onward. Nothing was big enough to halt its forward movement. The crack split the earth. Water poured in everywhere.

My side of the crack was moving away. The water was widening into a river, a lake—my God! the ocean! I was going out into the *ocean*! I made a giant leap and just made it to Bill's side. The side that had settled down. "Oh, Bill! *Bill*!"

"Honey, wake up! Wake up, honey!" Bill shouted as he shook my shoulders.

The terrible sights and sounds suddenly stopped. I was safe in my own bed. I was sweating. When I realized it was just a dream, I couldn't relax.

We got up and each had a cigarette.

I needed to calm down and analyze the dream.

We discussed it at length and when I was satisfied, we returned to bed.

The following day I asked my wise old friend about it. "I had a dream last night," I began.

"Summer dream every night."

"Yes, I know. But this was a lot different though."

"How this one different?"

"It was so real. I could see so clearly. Colors were brilliant. Movements were so...well, I felt every single movement. And that sound, that horrible groan, was like nothing I've ever heard, it was so loud."

She nodded and rocked hard.

"No-Eyes, I was *terrified*! It was so *real*! When Bill finally woke me up I was soaked with sweat."

"Summer say it so real."

"Yes. Yes, it was just like I was really there in that shop."

"Summer not know why it so real?"

I thought. I was stunned at the thought. Silence.

"Yep. Summer really there."

"My spirit, it went into the future."

"Yep."

"But why? I already knew what's coming."

"Summer *feel* what coming? Know and feel two separate stuff."

"Knowing is enough."

"Nope."

"But, No-Eyes, the people, they were in pieces—all broken and bloody. They screamed and screamed. They were stampeding over each other and . . . . "

"I know."

Silence. I was thinking of the horrors I'd witnessed.

"Now Summer know *and* feel."

"I'll never forget that terrible sound the crack made."

"Earth Mother hurt real bad."

"Yes, she was. She's going to be."

"That only bit of stuff."

"I don't think I want to talk about it."

"Seems Summer no want to talk 'bout many stuff!"

"Let's talk about something else."

"Nope."

"Why?"

"No can put head in dirt. Stuff come anyways. Summer no can hide. That not make stuff go away."

"I know that, No-Eyes. Please, not now."

Silence.

"Please?" I pleaded. Things were too vivid in my mind. I was too shaken and I just wanted to forget it—for now.

"Okay, but Summer remember, we gonna talk 'bout stuff again."

"Thanks." I sighed with relief. I knew the subject was most likely going to be another lesson. I sure didn't want it to be when the horrors were so fresh in my memory. I admired the old Chippewa for respecting my sensitive feelings.

"Summer bring up subject. We talk 'bout dreams."

"Bill's guide told us a lot about dreams, No-Eyes. Maybe we should discuss something he hasn't covered."

"Who teacher here?"

"I'm not, I just didn't want you wasting your time."

"I no waste time. He speak 'bout *all* things. What left for No-Eyes?"

"You add a different viewpoint to the subjects."

"That right. That why I no waste time. We speak 'bout dreams now."

"Alright."

"That better."

"Since you insist on this subject, I do have one gnawing question."

"What that?"

I thought a minute. I decided to play with her. "You tell *me* what my question is."

"What so! This game?"

"Yep." I teased.

She grinned. She didn't answer but looked hard at me. Her sightless eyes were dark mirrors reflecting my image.

I waited.

The grin widened. "Summer want know 'bout death dream."

"Good, very good. Now, what do I want to know about it?"

"This long game."

"Not so long."

Silence.

Waiting.

"Summer want know why death not happen."

"You're incredible." I laughed.

She laughed. "No. That just way stuff is. No magic. It nature."

"You're *still* amazing."

"Summer do same stuff one day."

I rolled my eyes as if to say, yeah sure.

"That no way to believe. Summer do stuff too."

"I already do. I just can't turn it on and off like you do."

"That come."

"What about the dream?"

"What dream?"

"No-Eyes!"

"Summer dream many times 'bout death finger pointing at Bill's tombstone. It have right birthdate. What so! It have death date. What so!"

"But the birthdate was exact! The death date was 1983! No-Eyes, I worried all that year about him dying! *All* my death dates have been accurate. What happened to his?"

"Summer make stuff stop."

"How could I? How did I?"

"Summer see year on tombstone. Summer see day too?"

"No, just the year. I saw that he would die in the blue truck. He went down a hill in winter. I worried every time he went out into the mountains."

"I tell Summer day he 'sposed to go. It December 31."

"That's New Year's!"

"Yep."

"I worried all year long and he wasn't supposed to die until the *last* day?"

"Yep."

"What stopped it?"

"Summer tell."

I thought. Bill did have a service call come in on New Year's Eve. It was snowing lightly. Mrs. Unser was having some trouble with her thermostat. Bill told her he'd be right out to replace it. He asked me if I wanted to ride along. I did. I often went with him on his calls. We loved being together. Mrs. Unser lives alone in a lovely house down on Ute Pass. Her drive is very steep and it was directly after a sharp turn on the Pass. We made the turn and started up the driveway. We got nearly to the top when the tires began to spin on the thick ice. The truck slid. Bill braked. The truck slid. It slid all the way back down to the highway and the oncoming traffic of the Pass. I had my door open and was watching while we were sliding backwards toward the highway. I was calm and unaware how nervous Bill had been. We came to a slow halt two feet from the busy highway.

"Summer see?"

"That's when he would've died?"

She nodded.

"But I was with him!"

"Yep. That change probability. *You* not ready to go then."

"You mean to tell me that he's alive just because I went with him that night?"

"Yep. Why Summer not scared when truck slide?"

"I don't know. Bill asked me the same thing. I had my door open and I was just watching us slide down. I had no thought that we wouldn't stop in time."

"Summer not think stuff like that because Summer work on truck. Summer stop truck."

"I didn't consciously. I wasn't applying any energies on the brakes."

"That not stuff Summer *think* 'bout. Summer do stuff by instinct."

"So I was doing it anyway. That's why I wasn't afraid." I was silent for a few minutes. I unconsciously directed my energies on the brakes. Then I thought of another incident that occurred while I was a secretary at a local real estate firm. I was sitting at my desk talking with an agent who appeared to have an interest in the paranormal. We were discussing an unusual sensation, a breeze, he occasionally experienced inside the store of his campground. Mike also said a presence could be detected elsewhere, in certain cabins. He was asking me if I would consider going out there and trying to locate the source and possibly identify it. While we were talking, the small hand calculator on the edge of my desk suddenly whisked off. I caught it just in time. Mike was amazed. "You did that with your mind, didn't you!" I laughed at the very idea. I excused it away, but he wasn't convinced. I inquired of No-Eyes on that now. "Did I ever move anything without realizing it?"

"What Summer think?"

Then I remembered other incidents. "Yeah, I did."

"Summer need to learn more control. Summer get excited and not learn to control energies when excited. Energies fly out in all directions, bump into stuff."

"Well, guess I'll have to be more aware of that. And I hope I don't have any more of those dreams, at least about Bill."

"Nope."

"How can you be so sure?"

"Bill use up all probabilities. He only have one left, last one."

"Can I ask when that is?"

"Summer can ask. I no tell."

"Why not?"

"It when Summer go too. It when all family ready to go."

"That's a relief!"

"What so! Why relief?"

"Because, and I'm assuming here, we've gone through a lot. We've got certain things to do. We're going to be here to guide and comfort. We won't go until many years from now. Tell me if I'm right."

Silence.

"Come on, No-Eyes, you can at least say that much. Am I right?"

She nodded.

Instant relief! I had been told by our friend that everyone has several designated possibilities for them to die. These are probabilities that are signposts along the wayside of our life's path. Since they are only possibilities and not concrete facts, there is room for changes. Evidently Bill was ready to approach one of his death signposts, but I wasn't. Therefore, because I was with him, his probability was changed and he was allowed to pass by it unharmed. I thank God I went with him that night.

"Thank you, No-Eyes."

"Humph. Summer get much out of No-Eyes that No-Eyes no mean to tell."

"That's because we're such good friends."

"Humph."

"Right?"

"Summer right." She sighed.

"Are we still going to talk about dreams?"

"Summer think No-Eyes change mind?"

"No."

"Good! Now, Summer dream all nights. Many dreams Summer's spirit go out to future. Summer see changes on Earth Mother. Many dreams Summer's spirit go out to past. Summer see playmate, Egyptian king. Many dreams Summer's spirit tell what wrong in life, tell who no good in life."

"Yes, but not always."

"Many dreams Summer think all mixed up."

"Yes, they're too jumbled to interpret."

"He teach Summer how to do that stuff?"

"Among other things, yes."

"Summer never ask him 'bout moving sky."

"No, I never did. Do you want to explain that one?"

"First tell of feelings."

"Well, I'll never forget it, that's for sure. I had it just after we moved to Colorado. No-Eyes, it was so beautiful. I saw the sky above me. It was night. There were no heavenly bodies; no moon, planets or stars. Instead, in a grand huge circle were the living undulating figures of the twelve zodiac signs. They were alive and shimmering with vibrant radiating colors. The entire astrological scene was beautiful beyond description. Then, it was gone. I woke up and lay for a long while desperately trying to maintain the incredible beauty of the vision."

"What feelings?"

"Beauty. All I could think of was how beautiful it was. I thought it was something special, but the beauty aspect of it was what remained with me."

"Summer have no other feelings?"

"I guess it comforted me. Yes, I felt a kind of peace settle through me."

She nodded and grinned.

I returned the smile.

"Summer so good when she interpret dreams of other peoples. Why Summer no see stuff in this one?"

"At the time, the time of the dream, we were really having a hard time of life. Bill couldn't find work and we had gone through most of the savings that was supposed to be used for our mountain land. We had to use that to live on. We were depressed and frustrated. I see now that the composite forces were giving comfort. Right?"

"Yep. What so! Comfort no good if Summer not see it until years later."

"Yeah." I thought about that. "Still, I did receive comfort from it. I often thought about the beautiful vision during the daytime. I thought about it many times."

"It work then."

"Yeah, it worked without me ever realizing it."

"That way stuff go."

"I guess. No-Eyes, Bill had a dream about his friend, Rick. He dreamed Rick would be in an accident where he'd badly injure his leg, around the knee. Has that probability passed?"

"What so?"

"If it hasn't, Bill will remind him again."

"No need. One time enough."

"Thanks."

"Peoples need know how to read dream stuff."

"That's another side of the coin."

"That what?"

"Sorry. That's a different matter."

"Summer tell peoples that stuff."

"It's not that simple, No-Eyes."

"It simple. Summer write book."

I laughed. Even though it wasn't really funny to me. "That definitely isn't easy."

"Summer writer, Summer write. That simple."

"No-Eyes, I can write until my hand drops off. In fact, I have. Writing is only the beginning. It's getting the writing into a book that's the hard part."

"Why? Many books to read."

"I've tried for years, No-Eyes, it's just not that simple. Thousands of writers are trying to get books printed. It's too hard. There's too many people trying."

"Summer can."

I sighed.

"Well?"

"Well besides, there's already several dream books out now."

"They right?"

"Only one that I know of."

"*One?* One book, that all?"

"Yeah, but the people can't tell which ones are right. I feel bad about that. They want to interpret their dreams and they have the wrong books to go by. They're using all the wrong symbology."

"Summer fix."

"I don't think so, No-Eyes. Why would they believe mine over another?"

"Summer's right! That why!"

"We seem to be back where we started. No-Eyes, they wouldn't know mine would be right."

"They know! They know here!" She pounded her chest.

Deep sigh. I dearly loved the old lady. We had problems. We had times, like now, when we clashed our heads like the mountain rams challenging each other. The sound of our etheric horns clashing was an almost audible echo bounding back and forth off her cabin walls. It was impossible for me to convince her of the massive competition of the publishing world. Perhaps she could see something I could not. However, I didn't doubt the possibility of me putting together a book based on her and my friends' dream symbology, what I did doubt was that I'd be able to ever get it published. I put the idea aside. I really had quite enough to do for now. I placated her. "I'll think about it."

"That not good enough."

"It'll have to do for now. Don't you think I've got enough things to do for awhile? My lessons here take up an awful lot of time."

"We speak other stuff."

"No-Eyes, you didn't answer me." This time I was the one pushing for an answer.

"We see. Maybe, maybe not."

That was eternally her vague way of saying that I was right—for now; but she was going to be right in the final analysis. I despised that left-up-in-the-air reply of hers.

"Okay. We'll go on then."

"What Summer want know now?"

"Aimee had a dream a few years ago. I want to know if I interpreted it right."

"What dream? Aimee dream many stuff."

"The one where she saw the rope come out of the wall and go back through."

"That no dream. She *see!*"

"Thanks. That's what I explained to her."

"She believe?"

"Sure she did. My kids aren't stupid."

"She tell many peoples?"

"'Course not! They know better."

"Good little ones. They lucky."

"I'm not so sure."

"What so *that* 'sposed to mean?"

"No-Eyes, a heck of a lot of people out there don't believe these special things. They don't believe the spirit has heritage abilities. When a child has these things she believes everyone knows about them. We've had to explain that a lot of people don't believe in them. The girls have to keep quiet about them. It's hard for youngsters."

"They still lucky. Think how world be if *all* little ones have gifts cared for. *Not* have stuff talked out of minds!"

"Yeah, it'd be a lot more aware, wouldn't it."

"Humph, peoples dumb."

"We're coming to that circle again, No-Eyes."

"We come to many circles, Summer. They stop some day."

"That'd be nice."

"It come. It no can help."

I'd like to believe she was referring to a general awakening of awareness in the minds of the public. I knew she was speaking about something much more grave than that. "I know. Can we talk about that later? You're working us around back to my dream."

"Summer know, huh."

"Sometimes you're very transparent."

"Summer know No-Eyes *too* good now."

"I could never know you too good. I don't think anybody could."

"Day come when Summer know enough stuff."

"I could learn all my life and still have more to learn."

"Summer learn from No-Eyes all No-Eyes can teach. Day come when No-Eyes done."

"You know so many wonderful things. You learn from so many beautiful sources. I'll always be able to learn more from you."

"Nope." She had a glint of sadness to her single word.

"Well then," I tried, "when my lessons are over I'll still come up here and we'll just visit like friends."

Silence.

I reached for the wrinkled brown hand. "No-Eyes, we'll always be friends, special friends. I'll come up here and we'll fly all day with that falcon!"

Silence.

"We'll go out and pick berries and then make jam! We'll join the beavers again! We'll go back into the sun! We'll..."

"Summer!" she cut me off.

I pulled back.

She softened. "Summer, I not always gonna be here."

"What do you mean? Where would you go?"

"No-Eyes get old, Summer." She was sad, yet sounded full of a complete acceptance.

"If that's all you're worried about, we can take care of you. You could come live with us! We'd take care of you."

Silence.

I searched hard into the dark misty pools. I looked in deep with more than my eyes. And what I saw filled my heart with a heaviness I've never known. It filled my spirit with a great emptiness. It filled my throat with a hard lump. I cried.

Journey by the Wayside

May you acknowledge the voice within,
And harken to its power and wisdom.

On one particularly spectacular autumn afternoon, I decided to make an impromptu trip out to visit No-Eyes. I pulled the truck off onto the granite gravel of the wayside several times during my drive in order to psychically assimilate the intense vibrations nature was freely emitting. The surrounding scenery was so acute in its beauty, it won the tug-of-war it had been playing with my senses. I had to stop to admire it. It well knew that it was attracting me by its ravishing charms and I acquiesced to its vanity.

The encircling hillsides were ablaze with the roaring inferno of autumn's most glorious display. It would appear that I was a microscopic being that had inadvertently stumbled upon a buccaneer's hidden treasure trove. I was entirely enveloped in a shimmering universe of riches far beyond any human's finite comprehension.

I cautiously picked my way down the mountainside to remove myself from the distractive sounds of the highway vehicles above me. When all was soundless, I rested among the deadfall of the forest floor and reverently entered into the mesmerizing entity of autumn.

I do not know whether autumn's spirit found and engulfed me like an all-consuming opalescent fog rolling inland, or whether I had discovered a secret entry point in its veil of sheer filament. The precise mechanics of it is, in the end, irrelevant to me. The absurdity of the esoteric feat alone was, to me, inscrutable. However, I've come to learn of the complete futility of trying to comprehend the intricate complexities of these psychic quirks of nature, instead, I've resorted to the simplistic attitude of acceptance.

As I willingly allowed nature to ingest my foreign presence within her being, I sensed a certain inaudible communication with an all-pervasive force. This unnamed power was evidenced by a bizarre predominance of sensual lightheadedness. It was as though my entire being was expanding outward in all directions. It was as though my limited mind had an instantaneous metamorphosis into a vast expanse of fullness, a fullness that greatly amplified my hearing and magnified my vision. I soon discovered this sensation to be total awareness.

I opened my eyes and found the presence still within me. The glory I envisioned before me was no match for mere words. No adjectives could even near compare to the total beauty of the spectacle before me.

Entire mountainsides writhed in their undulating colors. The aspens, in their climax, illuminated the shimmering atmosphere with their brilliance. Ruby reds flared through jewels of amethyst and golden beryl leaves. The tall evergreens were scattered about like so many glimmering gems of jade. The intermittent shadows reflected about like dancing slivers of hematite. Together, they joined their efforts and orchestrated a symphony of living vibrations that radiated its gilded spires up into the receiving turquoise sky.

Far down in the narrow valley below me, all of life was an ever-changing kaleidoscope of quivering vibrations. The meandering stream snaked its somnambulating way through the dense waterway bushes and undergrowth. The blinding sun powerfully touched upon the water's surface, releasing brilliant diamond droplets to disperse through the wavering air. At some specifically designed invisible point, these delicate droplets shattered like translucent crystal and fell, tinkling like temple bells, back upon a waiting carpet of emerald loam.

The balmy autumn breeze touched my being in a dozen different places. It did not brush against me all at once as was usual. I examined this and found the wind to be a compilation of a million whispers of air, all trying to initiate me into the secrets of nature. I listened with strained intent, yet my unconditioned mind could not differentiate their individual meanings. I accepted these offerings of wisdom, ignorant as I was of their totality, and suddenly found myself once again, unto myself. I had somehow found my way back on the outside of reality. I had seen reality and my everyday life was most assuredly lived on the outside of it. The breeze that warmed my face was once again whole and representative of a normal halcyon autumn day in the mountains.

As I drove toward No-Eyes' cabin, I didn't bother to sort out what had happened to me back there on the quiet mountainside. If I really wanted to know, I knew that No-Eyes would have the appropriate explanation. I wasn't even convinced that I was going to tell her about my mystical union with nature. I wasn't sure I'd tell anyone at all. Right now, all I cared about was reveling in the residual feeling of exhilaration left from my experience. I was on a psychic high. Maybe that was my first official encounter with a Rocky Mountain High. Whatever it was, whatever had caused it, I wanted to find it again, and again.

I parked the truck in my usual spot and hummed a John Denver tune as my feet nearly pranced to the door of No-Eyes. She was nowhere around outside and I gently rapped on her door. She called me inside. "Come Summer, what delayed you?"

My heart sank like lead in water as I realized that my private happening was probably common knowledge to the old wise one. I tested the air. "Oh, I just stopped to take in the autumn colors. You knew I was coming, though, didn't you?"

No-Eyes didn't even look my way, instead she continued her knitting without the slightest pause. "No-Eyes hear mountain. No-Eyes hear what whispered, that all."

I pushed farther. "And tell me, old one, did the mountain tell you anything else?"

Still the creak and thud of her rocker continued without skipping its incongruous beat. Still she continued her knitting without glancing toward me. "What more to hear, huh, Summer? What more for mountain to say?"

I sighed a silent breath of relief. Her mystical line of gossip had been incomplete this time. My secret was still safe. I looked to her again and she was sightlessly staring at me, the incessant clicking of her rapid needles poised in mid-stitch, the rocker statue-still. We froze in time. She grinned and continued her work. "Summer mad mountain spoil surprise, huh Summer?"

For a split second I thought she was concealing the fact that she really did know of my secret. Then, when she spoke, I realized she was referring to my surprise visit. "Well, I am a little disappointed," I replied.

She tenderly put away her work and motioned for me to sit beside her. I pulled up an over-stuffed chair and settled in. She immediately changed the subject at hand and began my next lesson. When the old Chippewa talked, she was as animated as a Walt

Disney cartoon. Her expressions always served to emphasize her words, and even though her eyes were sightless, they sparkled and danced in time to her narration. "Today Summer learn of island inside you."

"But you already told me all about that." I quickly reminded.

No-Eyes' face turned somber. Her wispy brows pulled down to form a gray vee. She pursed her thin lips and slapped her hand on the arm of the rocker. "Summer! I know what already said!"

I apologized for having so rudely interrupted her. I was ashamed for having inferred that she was going to repeat a lesson. No-Eyes never repeated herself unless I specifically requested a clarification on a particular point I was having difficulty grasping. "I'm sorry, old one. I'm really sorry. I guess I was just anxious."

Her scowl smoothed out and the power behind her eyes softened. "You too anxious too much time. You need patience lesson. Not now, now Summer hear of island inside." She pounded her chest with one boney-fisted hand. The lesson began. She the instructor, with the ancient wisdom in her head, and me the learner, trying desperately to get it all into mine.

For the sake of easier reading and better comprehension of No-Eyes' words, I will write her lesson in my own manner of speaking.

Long ago, many many moons ago, the Great Spirit was lonely. He felt so alone, so alone that He decided to create some company. This company would give Him great comfort, respect and love. First the Great Spirit created the lights in the heavens. He then went on to fashion all life on these lights. Some lights had no life, but many did. The Great Spirit wanted something more like Himself. He shuddered. As He made this grand movement, millions of sparkles flashed out from His glowing Being. These sparkles were minute images of Himself. He was pleased that He had created in His image and He rested and watched.

These sparkles of the Great Spirit were spirits, spirits of God. These spirits wandered around for years and years, eventually becoming bored. They saw the animals having physical sensations and were displeased and jealous over this lack on their part. They thought that if they could enter into these animals, then they too could enjoy the physical bodies as the animals did.

The first Great Sin was committed.

Many monstrous creatures now roamed the planet. Cats with fins, unicorns, horses with wings, all manner of mixtures prevailed. The spirits knew they had done a grave wrong, but they had no power to correct it.

The Great Spirit looked down and was angered. He then took common dirt and fashioned five men of five differing colors. He then created mates for them and said, "Go and spread out upon the land. I have given you life. I give to you all knowledge to make nations of yourselves. Go and purify the lands your brothers have desecrated. You will live according to my laws. Your spirits can never return unto me until they themselves have returned to the land many times and are purified."

So God had fashioned five human forms in brown, red, black, yellow and white skin colors. The men took their women and traveled far over the lands, spreading out to settle and form nations of people. Eventually, through the gift of wisdom, all the monstrous self-creations were transformed into the human form.

Civilizations quickly evolved and technology rapidly developed. It advanced so fast that the people were becoming envious of other nations' knowledge. Soon the advancement had reached its pinnacle in the development of a great crystal that could power an entire nation. This crystal was to be their eventual downfall as it broke the lands up and vanished the civilizations.

The Great Spirit was again angered and chose one pure family out of each of the five nations. He gave them explicit instructions and then sent waters over all the land. The five pure families had saved all manner of wildlife and when the waters receded, new nations were begun again.

I was fascinated at No-Eyes' tale. Surely this was far removed from the typical Indian stories I had read. I asked her where she heard it and, even more puzzling to me, why she believed it.

"Mountain Spirit tell me long ago. Mountains not lie. No-Eyes know it true—wind say so."

Then the old woman explained about how the spirit of the Great Spirit lives in every human being. She went into great animation and detail about why we must live our lives according to the Great Spirit's laws.

Every person on Earth must be born again in order to re-enter God's spirit for all eternity. Since the Great Sin was committed, we all have that stain on our spirits and it must be totally eradicated in order to be pure. That is only the tip of the problem though. In order to be born again, our spirits, which never die, must continue being reborn in physical human bodies in order to balance out all impure stains from the previous lifetime. In other words, No-Eyes was talking reincarnation of the spirit. The balance-of-payments was the sole criterion for re-entering into the Being of God, or heaven. She explained that if a slave trader lived a life of cruelty in one lifetime, then that spirit would return as a black person in its next lifetime to balance out its wrong doing. This theory of balance-of-payments, some call karma. She herself just referred to it as "the balance." She said that whatever gift or characteristic is misused, it will be misused on you in the next life. No-Eyes made reference to a Great Book of Records that contains the entire accountability of every spirit since their original creation. I remembered reading about reincarnation and posed a question to her that I had heard others ask. "If all the original spirits God created never die, why aren't there more people on Earth?"

She flashed me her wonderful toothless smile and understandably replied, "Think Summer, think. Many spirits pure and complete. Many pure everyday. They happy in Great Spirit."

She said that thousands of spirits are done with "the balance" and continue to exist in their own dimension. Those completed ones help and serve as guardians to those still in the physical world. Also, she said that more people are here now because more and more near-pure spirits wish to help here on Earth rather from the invisible side of reality.

No-Eyes then taught about the shrewdness of listening to your inner spirit, the very essence of the Great Spirit.

Within every living human being throbs the shining light of a spirit, God's spirit. That makes us a part of God and our physical bodies are only an encasement, or vehicle. The spirit is the reality of a person. It is the only portion that lives on after the casing dies away. The body is only superficial; however, because it houses a portion of the Great Spirit, it should be cared for reverently like a church's holy tabernacle. When the physical body dies, it is like sloughing off an old dead skin. That which is left, the remaining life and vitality of the spirit, is totally alive and aware. That spirit is the sum total of all the physical personalities it possessed. The dead body is now nothing more than a wrecked car is, littering up a junkyard. No-Eyes said the most efficient way to dispose of it was by burning. She didn't understand the logic of why we insist on using up good land for dead bodies. The real person, the spirit, is still alive. The living spirit is the body's real life and personality.

I told No-Eyes that people wanted to bury their dead out of respect for the body that housed the spirit within. She didn't buy that. "They do not understand," she said sadly.

No-Eyes perked up and slapped my knee. "Why Summer come here?" she suddenly asked of me.

"I come here because I like being with you. You always have such wonderful things to teach me," I answered happily.

"Not here!" she said rather sharply as she pointed to her floor, "Here to mountains!" She extended her thin arms about the small room.

I couldn't tell her exactly why we sold everything, left all our family behind and came to the unknown mountains. I attempted to explain. "We came because we had to."

"That no answer. Who tell Summer had to?" she persisted.

"Nobody told us. We just had to come." I attempted again.

"Think Summer, think!" she ordered.

I just despised it when she said that to me, and she said it often. It was a request, yet an order. I thought. I thought back on that time almost eight years ago. I remembered that once Bill and I made the final decision to leave, any further deviations from that set course seemed to be entirely out of our jurisdiction. It appeared that it was completely out of our hands. Our future path was set in motion. The final decree was handed down and it was not revocable, nor was it retrofitted with boosters to accommodate a reverse thrust.

"We told ourselves we had to come here." I tried.

"Who you?" she queried.

"Bill and I, us!" I replied defensively.

"Who Bill? Who you?" she insisted.

Then her line of questioning finally led me to her point. "We're spirits," I answered proudly.

No-Eyes grinned. "Took Summer long to come up with that one." she laughed.

I sheepishly agreed. I hated it when I'd let her biting questions rattle me so. At times I could barely think straight. Yet she had all the time in the world for me to calm down my mind and to turn it into an intelligent and logical computer.

The lesson continued.

No-Eyes' question led to a dissertation on following the wisdom of the spirit within. The spirit knows best, she'd say. The old woman told me that our spirits wanted us to be surrounded by the pure and innocent vibrations of nature, specifically, the mountains.

Well, I had already felt a real love for mountains and forests, even living in Detroit. I had always dreamed of someday living in them, but that was forever and logically considered just that, a dream.

No-Eyes then likened our spirits to islands within us, islands of the Great Spirit. She said that the island within each of us speaks to us all the time, but hardly anyone ever listens to it. They shut it off and out of their logical thinking, even out of their lives. Anyone, everyone can do whatever they feel is right for them to do. That inner island, that spirit, makes each person a total and separate individual. Everyone came here for a specific purpose. An extremely important purpose chosen by the spirit. That spirit directs the physical mind toward the most efficient method of achieving its intended goal. If we don't listen to the promptings of the spirit, then we will most likely not attain our mission here and this entire lifetime will have been wasted, as far as "the balance" for the spirit is concerned.

The old woman stressed the utmost importance on doing what is best for your spirit's attainment-to-completion. Since the spirit is the true essence of your being, its goals are more important than the physical wants and goals of the mind or body. Only the spirit and its spiritual acquisitions survive physical death.

She illustrated my own situation back eight years ago, when our families, friends and neighbors couldn't fathom why we would want to leave a positive future and all our acquired belongings for an uncertain future and nothing to call our own. She reminded me of the tears and hard feelings we caused by our decision to leave everyone and everything. Yet, she said we were inwardly compelled to follow the voice of our spirits, even though we had nothing and didn't know where we would end up.

No-Eyes finished the lesson.

If everyone could only grasp the simple fact that they alone are their own keeper. Only they have total control over their own destiny. Nothing should interfere with their spirit's promptings. In the end, each spirit must account for its failure, whether that failure-of-purpose be caused from family, material goods, social or business position or from fear of ridicule; makes no difference. You alone must answer for your own deaf ear. You alone must find the courage to live your life according to your spirit. Find the strength to leave the material things behind. You can't lead your life as others expect you should and still be that wonderful individual island inside. Don't listen to how others tell you to lead your life. Listen to the Great Spirit within. Don't listen to those who say you can't do this or you can't do that just because you'd be striking away from the norm. Listen to the Great Spirit within. Don't be afraid to be different. Don't be hampered by unaware ridicule. Don't be swayed by customs of mere men when you could be listening to the Great Spirit within. You are a universe unto yourself and God is its living core.

I understood all No-Eyes told me this day and gratefully thanked her for being so patient with all of my questions. As I was preparing to leave her cozy home, I reached for her door and opened it. "Thanks again, old one. See you soon."

She had returned to her knitting and rocking. Without looking up toward the door, she calmly said, "Bye Summer, good happening on mountain, shows you coming along."

My heart really did sink this time. The old woman knew of my secret all along. Well, who could be angry at a lone, blind woman. I smiled and gently closed the door on the darkness inside that was brightly illuminated by an old woman's mind.

Song of the Shaman

May the wings of visions flutter softly,
And may your Spirit perceive
their message.

Autumn is my favorite time of year. All of nature is going all out in a final celebration of life before its long season of hibernation. The mountainsides are an inferno of color. The quickened breezes gradually gain in momentum to blow miniature tornados of reds and golds across the highway. Swirling leaves play a wild and ferocious game of tag with the wind. Woodsmoke permeates the chilled air with an intoxicating incense. Autumn has arrived to steal the show. Once again she has successfully upstaged summer, the former bit player, on life's mighty stage. Her brilliant costumes become more elaborate with each passing year. She demands a building excitement from her captive audience. She demands to be noticed and raved about. She demands all of these because she knows she is resplendent in her unequalled beauty. She is truly unsurpassed. And she never fails to receive her standing ovations. She graciously drapes her fast-fading robes about her and bends low in her final bow.

I was in a high-spirited mood as I drove through the twisting masses of leaves on my way to No-Eyes' cabin. The air was heavy with woodsy smells, smells that always make me think of sitting with a loved one in front of a roaring fire while the wind raps angrily on our windows. Autumn excited my senses, often to the hazardous point of dulling my logic. Whenever I would do something less than intelligent, Bill would always remind me that fall wasn't here yet. That's alright, everyone has their mental "down times." Autumn just happens to be mine. I'm too busy being drunk with the highly intoxicating nectar of nature in its glory.

The day was sunny, yet chilly. I wondered why No-Eyes hadn't built a fire inside. There was an odd absence of spiraling smoke from her yawning chimney.

I worried. I ran up the hill and entered the tomb-like darkness.

A low chanting came from the far corner of the main room. I quietly closed the door behind me and waited until my eyes adjusted. The monotone chanting continued without a break in its lazy rhythm. I peered through the semi-darkness and saw No-Eyes sitting cross legged on the bare pine floor. She was rocking back and forth like a silent metronome set on slow timing. I remained as still as a cat waiting for its juicy mouse to appear.

"Summer sit," she whispered.

I sat down across from her on the floor.

"Not there!" she croaked angrily. "Somebody already there!"

I scrambled up and sat on the couch. Evidently the old one was entertaining someone again. I had stupidly forgotten about her frequent unseen friends. The chanting stopped abruptly and I watched her animated silence. She would nod or shake her head depending on whether or not she agreed with what was transpiring in the inaudible conversation. I felt rather like the proverbial odd man out.

"Summer belong," she whispered.

I nodded in a dubious acknowledgement.

"We *all* belong!" she repeated emphatically.

"Yes, old one," I acquiesced.

Silence again as the conversation continued. I thought, "I belong. I belong. I belong." Yet, how could I possibly belong when I couldn't hear what was being said? Or see who was saying what?

The old woman slowly opened her huge sightless eyes and patted the floor, indicating that I could now sit across from her.

"Come. It okay now."

I sat cross-legged and wondered how she could remain in that strained position for so long.

"It easy. Old bones used to it."

I grinned, trying to hide the embarrassment of my thought. We sat in the heavy silence for several minutes. Perhaps she was collecting and collating her thoughts. Perhaps she was simply resting between conversations. I know what I was doing. I was shivering.

"Summer scared?"

"No, I'm not scared. I'm cold! You should have your fire going in here. I'll just...."

"Sit!"

I settled back down and faced her.

"Summer lazy! Summer make *herself* warm!"

I signed. I guess I was lazy. I'm guilty as charged. No-Eyes had nearly exhausted herself bringing me through difficult lessons of mental body control. I had successfully learned how to rid myself of headaches without the use of drugs. I had mastered the control of my anxiety (impatience), which had been causing me some serious physical problems. I had learned to lessen pain in myself and others. However, cooling and warming the skin surface still took a great deal of mental energy, more than I usually wanted to take the time to expend. I knew she now wanted me to do this. And I hated it. Why couldn't we just build a nice cozy fire and forget it? Of course her basic reply would be that everything comes easier with practice.

I boldly heaved out an exasperated sigh, readjusted my position, closed my eyes and began the laborious process of warming myself. I don't know how long I took this time, but I was as warm as if I'd built that fire.

"That better." the old woman said softly.

"Yes," I whispered.

"Next time Summer come, you hear my friends."

"I'm not ready for that yet, No-Eyes. I really do think I need more time before I can do that."

We spoke in hushed tones whenever we were in a lesson situation.

"Who teacher here?"

"You are."

"You bet!"

"But shouldn't I feel a readiness? Shouldn't I know too?"

"Summer, if everybody wait 'til they think they ready, nobody go anywhere."

"Still...."

"No still. You have to jump in. Try."

"I don't know...."

"Who teacher here?"

Silence from me.

"Summer not paid to know. I know. That enough!"

"Alright" was all I could manage. It was nearly impossible to argue with her. In the final analysis, she was always right.

"Summer shake autumn out of head. Be aware!"

"I am aware!" I barked disrespectfully.

"Not in autumn," she said, having the final word.

I sighed. I spent a lot of time sighing.

There was no fooling one such as No-Eyes. She could read you like braille. Nothing, absolutely nothing, slipped past her fine mind. She was incredible. That was what kept me coming back time after time. She would expose your raw, ugly faults and show you how to correct them. She was undaunted by defensive dishonesty. Instead, she would weave around it and, in the end, let you know she'd known the truth all along. This readily cured anyone of a white lie, no matter how white it was.

"Summer still warm?"

"Yes."

"Summer clear head?"

"Yes," I whispered back with a grin.

"Summer think something funny?"

"Yes, No-Eyes, I do. I think you can be very funny."

"Good! I like you too."

The chilly cabin warmed with our friendship. We both understood each other perfectly. We remained silent while we wound down our humorous attitudes. When I was completely without emotion and thought, she spoke.

"Today Summer hear of No-Eyes."

My heart palpitated with an audible lunge. I had waited a long time to learn about this wizened Chippewa woman. I had reams of paper at home filled with questions I had wanted answers to. I thought about them and wished I had them with me now.

"No need papers. Summer read from here."

Oh God, she was so believing in me.

"I can't," I replied defensively.

"Can't? That not one of our words, Summer."

"I can't," I repeated.

"See papers in front of you," she ordered.

I did.

"Now, what first question?"

"Who are you? I asked, amazed that I was actually mentally seeing my handwritten questions.

"See! Summer *can*!"

"But I won't be able to see *all* my questions!"

"Summer *can*! Summer *will*! *Now*!"

And I did.

I learned a great deal about the old lone woman. I learned many things that were extremely private to her. I'm not quite convinced of her reasoning for revealing it all to me, only time will bear her out on that aspect. One thing was vividly clear though, I had been given an amazing amount of food for thought.

After all my questions were more than satisfactorily answered, I was allowed to build that fire. No-Eyes relaxed in her rocker and I pulled the large chair over in front of her. Our conversation became casual as we sipped on her special herbal tea blend. The general subject matter was soon beginning to narrow into specifics. I had picked a sensitive chord on the harp of her delicate spirit, ecology.

I had merely made an off-the-cuff remark regarding the unavailability of decent raw land. I had said that all the good stuff was divided and subdivided into tiny lots which were cluttered with so many covenants that a person could barely call it their own.

No-Eyes immediately became solemn. A dark curtain seemed to have been drawn over her light mood. She bowed her small head and fumbled with her fingers. I sensed a gross thickness in the atmosphere around us. I could feel the heaviness of some mournful pressure emitting from the old woman.

The fire was dancing in a wild and feverish blaze. Yet, the room was alive with a palpable presence. It heaved its icy breath through to my bones, as if I were some transparent fabric of gauze. The noonday sun had escaped behind a passing thunderhead and the cabin was plunged into foreboding shadows. The once gentle breeze had gained in force and was eerily scraping branches against the windows. A common autumn storm was evident. I looked to the still form of No-Eyes and wondered what etheric storm was brewing around us inside the cabin.

I sensed no fear. I sensed no evil or harmful intruder. What I was feeling was an extraordinary depression. A depression comprised of great sorrow and total defeat. This negative mixture of emotions caused an unbelievable draw on my energies. It was so magnetic it was bringing me down into its black quagmire. I visibly jerked my body upright and forced my mind to respond to a psychic counter-action. I mentally flashed up my protection and fortified it with powerful defenses.

The negative charge remained hovering about the room. Yet, I was now separated from it. It was as though I had a bubble of bullet-proof glass surrounding me. I was now unaffected. I leaned forward and held the frail hands of No-Eyes. She sadly looked up at me, then smiled.

The threatening atmosphere shattered like so many broken shards of porcelain. Outside, the storm raged on. Inside, it was once again quiet, warm and friendly.

"What was here?" I asked softly.

"Summer not know?" she whispered.

I thought before I answered her.

"I know it had everything to do with you. You caused the great sadness in this room. And it must've been because of what I was saying about land. Did I hurt you, old one?"

"Summer only half right."

I waited.

"*We* make that force. You, me, we are People of the Land. Land in our heart and spirit. No can separate."

"But how did I make it?"

"No-Eyes make it with sadness. Summer make it worse with desire."

I understood her meaning. She couldn't have stated it more plainly. The old woman was deeply saddened because the land of her people was stolen from them. She harbors a tremendous grudge. She holds this deep inside her until it explodes like a herd of a thousand buffalo charging across the Great Plains. I harbor a consuming desire to live freely on the land. Land that has not been bought by someone else. Someone who feeds his insatiable ego by devising ridiculous rules and covenants to rule the people who will purchase his land. My opinion of such covenants is strong. They are nothing more than restrictions, not protections. I want acres of land where I can live in total freedom with my family. And these two intense feelings of ours fed the negative force and gave it its life.

"I'm sorry, No-Eyes. I didn't mean to hurt you. We'll talk about something else," I offered sympathetically.

She patted my hand before leaning back into her chair. She was calm. She was gracefully resigned to those things which can never be changed.

"No Summer, now good time. We talk. We speak of it. I tell you true story."

"I just don't want to see you in pain. Couldn't we do this another time?"

"No other time like this time."

I curled my feet under me and prepared myself for her tale.

"Summer not know joy of real land. Not mean tiny bits like today. Today they make lines, cut up, scar Mother Earth. Today not same like yesterday. Yesterday our people lived free. We take only what we need, no more. We love the Mother our Earth. We care for her. When we take, we put back. Our people take animals for food, clothing and utensils. We first ask spirit of animal for forgiveness. Our people roam the land, not use it all up. We do not cut it up and leave her bare. We love Mother Earth, she good to us. We grateful.

"We teach babies to love Mother Earth. We teach words of nature. We hear mountains whisper. We hear animals tell many old secrets. All these good medicine for our people. We live in peace. People make all food and all medicine from Mother Earth's breast. She give us all needs. We no want more. What more to want?"

I studied No-Eyes as she told of the glorious days before the White Man. Her eyes sparkled with excitement. Her grin was wide and beaming. She made animated motions with her arms and hands. She was filled with a bursting love for a lost way of life.

I laughed at her youthful exuberance. She had a definite way of drawing me into the scene of whatever she was talking about. She had drawn me in and my heart leaped with the beauty of her painting. It was serene and idyllic. As she explained the People's daily life, she was meticulous in including every explicit detail. She told of the courtship rituals and the week-long marriage ceremonies. She explained the methods of birthing, which sounded more natural than the antiquated techniques of today. She invited me on a hunt and succeeded in making me believe I was actually there. We picked berries, tanned hides, prepared meals and washed our children with sand in the creek. We made exquisite jewelry creations and sewed warm buffalo robes for our men. I listened in on council talks and marvelled at the wisdom of the leaders. It was a beautiful life of respect, giving and sharing, caring and love. It was free.

No-Eyes had purposely led me into the magnificent tapestry. I was high on my involvement. I was mentally living the life of my ancestral grandmother's childhood days. And it felt so good.

This was one of the old woman's most powerful psychic lessons so far. I witnessed a woman's final throes of labor. I saw her crouch over the tiny fur-covered blanket. And I heard her cry of joy as it mingled with the squeal of her newborn son. I witnessed a secret council meeting. And I inhaled the smoke of the council pipe as it was passed full circle. I witnessed the tale of the storyteller. And I felt the love and excitement of all the small children gathered around his aged lap. I witnessed a family's lodge at night. And I was comforted by the togetherness I felt as they all slept peacefully on warm fur blankets. I witnessed a marriage lodge. And was moved by the tender love and respect I found therein. I was one of the People. And it was a beautiful way of being. It was a way of life that made the Great Spirit glad He created Man.

No-Eyes then dropped her tone like a lead weight. She nervously folded and refolded her worn handkerchief. Her facial expression of glowing excitement turned suddenly to deadpan. She reminded me of a mime in mid-performance.

"Then White Man come to People's land. He say land his. He say People go away. We say Mother Earth all man's land. Mother Earth good to all. He want to make lines, cut her up, scar her bountiful breast. He say People go or they kill People. We fight for our home. People live long time with Mother Earth. She been good to us. Our men try hard to keep them away. Our men try hard to protect women and children. When our men away on hunts, white men come burn down lodges, shoot women and children. Our men come back. They hurt and sad. They plenty angry. Many war councils send men out to stop whites. Whites have powerful guns. We get some. Whites get better guns. We cannot get those. Soon all buffalo gone. White men kill for hides. They leave good meat for vultures. Whole valleys, whole plains stink with wasted meat. Mother Earth cry. Our People cry. We move. We move again. They find us. We have no more land to move to. They trade land for blankets. Blankets got smallpox on them. We die like flies. White men bring People more presents. People's women and children die of cholera. White men say we can have much land to live on. We move to barren plains. They say they give us food. Flour have bugs. Meat have maggots. We prisoners on gift land. It no good for snakes even. White men multiply like rabbits. They too many for us. Finally last chief give up. He ride off of Staked Plains. He still plenty proud.

"Today People still on gift lands. One gift land white men give the People, they make test site for their bombs. They still taking. It never end. They Indian givers. They give, they grab back, say they never gave. White words no good then. They no good now. Nothing change. They still cut up Mother Earth.

"Summer, you will find dream land. Summer have good man. Summer have special mind. Summer have Medicine Woman in her. I Medicine Woman. I know these things. One day you have many come to Summer's land. They come to learn old ways. Summer and man teach. Summer not forget old ways. Summer not forget song of Shaman."

When No-Eyes was finished, I was crying like a hurt child. Her story had moved me so. I had felt the total fear of the People when they realized the white men were going to force them to leave their beloved lands. I felt the horror of the massacres of thousands of Indian women and children. I felt the blind hatred the Indian men had for the whites because of the senseless slaughter of their families.

No-Eyes' sadness had been transferred to me as efficiently as nourishment is passed through the umbilical cord from mother to fetus. She had given me something of herself, something of my heritage. A memory.

I knelt next to the old woman and rested my head on her lap. She stroked my hair.

"It not so bad, Summer. All peoples have pain. Some bad, some worse. You have good man to help. He understand. Summer be okay."

I looked into No-Eyes' face. She was staring at the wall behind me. A lone tear was leaving a glistening trace over its worn and tired trail.

A Breed Apart

May your life be blessed with the
greatest treasure,
And may you cherish and protect it
with reverence.

Bill and I shared a unique and beautiful bond. I do not refer here to marriage, although that is indeed an intangible bond, a bond that has increased in strength at each of our nineteen years of marriage. I do not speak here of love either, for we indeed have plenty of that anyway. Nor do I speak of understanding, for what is a good marriage or love without understanding? They are inseparable for a successful and lasting union to last through the trials of life. Our special bond, our greatest treasure, is simply nothing more than friendship. Yes, friendship. What is friendship? Friendship is a way of interacting between two people. It is being able to say things to one another without tip-toeing nervously about and around. It is total and complete honesty—in *all* things. It is being able to talk truthfully about feelings and faults. Friendship is showing deep understanding. It is standing loyally by. It is always being there to comfort and sympathize. It is being able to put aside your own depression in order to be optimistic for the other. It is always wanting to be together, to do things together, to share. Friends take joy in sharing the simple pleasures; walking through mist-filled woods, trying to spy a moving object together in the crystal timepiece of a summer's night sky, listening for native mountain voices. Friendship is all these beautiful things and, best of all, it was our bond.

This bond was cemented firmly in place by a unique recognition of spirits. All the world desperately tried all their many ingenious ploys to break up the awful love affair of two determined teenagers. All the world tried to wear down the edges of love of their young marriage. All the trials and hardships of life came uninvited into the marriage, trying forcefully to wedge the two apart. All the negative forces of nature drifted around the two, but never managing to break through into the bond. All of these adverse conditions were only to contribute to the ever-solid bond of love, understanding and friendship. The two were as an island, unreachable and untouchable by negative forces. And together they boldly searched for truth and found it. Together they confronted the skeptics and won. Together they confidently followed their path and found their purpose. Together they live in the comfort that the knowledge that the truth brings, and they are finally at their path's destination.

We are as one single spirit that had divided and split in two in order to enter two physical bodies. We are of one mind and one goal, to reach the point where we will be actually physically busy with our purpose. That is forever uppermost in our consciousness. Our daily lives are filled with waiting for the moment we will be about our business. And we are anxious—for time is indeed running out.

Since meeting the old Chippewa, we have been given a ray of hope to our goal. She has lent credence to our urgings. She has greatly lessened the pressure that time had levied on our restless spirits. Can I authoritatively state exactly who No-Eyes is? Probably not. Yet, our spirits recognize a certain innate quality in the old woman. We feel more than see what has brought our paths together at the most crucial point in time for us. We were no longer seeking. That beginner's aspect of spirituality was long ago over for us. Yet, we did desperately thirst for a spiritual kinship. Our fellowmen were good and had a surface friendliness. However, we were ever surrounded by the unaware, those who sought wealth and success. We were continually surrounded by those people who only saw the "I's" to life, the self-seeking, the egotistical. And so, the more alone we became, floating on the ocean of humanity.

The freshness of autumn was still with us. This, my favorite time of year. Bill and I had come so far during my time spent with the old woman. We were happy and content in the knowledge and insights we had gained from her. Each lesson I had with No-Eyes was an enlightening experience. I loved just being with her. Many of our days together were spent in doing general chores such as gathering wayside herbs. We would chatter like schoolgirls as we made jams from the local growing berries or mixed together a medicinal home remedy. Yet, even those carefree days were not wasted. She forever worked in a lesson. These lessons were not always spiritual in content. Many of them were regarding living the simple life that the Great Spirit planned for His people. She talked at length about the right way to live one's mental life, things like acceptance and continual perseverance were constantly woven through our general discussions.

I thought about all those wonderful days we spent together as I drove the truck under the sun-touched arches over my mountain road. The transparent rays slanted down through the quivering aspens and made one feel as if they were driving through the thin veil between dimensions. Heady woodsmoke drifted through the crisp mountain air. I loved that autumn fragrance. That scent alone brought a myriad of visions into my receptive mind, visions of walking through the forest and hearing the crunch of newly-fallen leaves underfoot, visions of the early autumn morning mist rolling gently through the valley below, visions of snuggling warmly in front of the blazing fire in our darkened living room. I loved autumn and today was perfect.

As I drove through the twisting mountain road to the old woman's cabin, I laughed at the joyful movements the leaves made as they danced on the wind before me. Their golden costumes swirled, made momentary pirouettes and then were swiftly swept off their stage. Their attentive audience of roadside trees swayed in time with nature's festive tune. And my heart was filled with their beautiful essence. Above me, the high winds were whipping up the rich white clouds into creamy soft lengths of taffy, stirring here and pulling away there. Everywhere I looked was the glorious proven evidence of God.

No-Eyes was bringing in a newly-split bundle of wood when I arrived. I helped her stack the scented wood beside her massive stone fireplace. The sweet aroma of pine filled our cozy schoolroom.

"It's gorgeous out today, No-Eyes."

"Yep. It that alright. Great Spirit happy today."

"I am too. I just love autumn."

She gave me a peculiar look.

"Well, I do!" I insisted.

"Autumn make Summer's head full of woodsmoke."

"That's just the way it is. Seems it's been that way for years."

"Summer no can think through woodsmoke. Lessons no good in autumn time."

"You're not being fair. I'm not that bad. Am I?"

"Almost." She grinned and pulled her rocker up to the couch.

I sat on the couch across from her. We were nearly knee to knee.

"We no have real lesson today. We gonna just talk."

"Good. I like it when we just talk."

She began rocking—hard.

Oh boy! Here comes a "talk" I'm not looking forward to.

Her voice was low and soft, "Summer, we gonna have to talk now."

I nodded and fumbled with my fingers.

"No-Eyes let Summer put off long enough."

"I know." I admitted sheepishly.

"Sit back. I gonna talk first."

I sat back into the low couch and pulled up my knees.

"Summer know 'bout purpose. We been into that stuff. Maybe Summer not know 'bout other people's purpose. We see. Many, many spirits here now, Summer. They here to bring special knowledge, special hope, special comfort and light to coming darkness days of all peoples."

"The changes, right?"

"No, Summer. Before that even—now. It no gonna be good later. That be too late. Changes come, no more New York, no more books, no more T.V.—radio even. Peoples here to give comfort, make peoples ready *now*. Summer, all over many new peoples here. Not only in mountains, that tiny part. Many new peoples all over country, other countries, other planets even. This gonna be big stuff, Summer. It gonna go on *all* over. Summer think Great Spirit only gonna come here? Summer think Great Spirit gonna fight evil ones only here? He gonna get rid of evil *all* over! This important here. Great Spirit gonna come after many big changes on Earth Mother, after many big changes *all* places. We not only planet! We talk 'bout great happening all over!"

I was listening to the grand scale she painted. This certainly was a big happening, bigger than I keep thinking.

"Many, many more new spirits coming here all time. Every day new spirits coming to prepare peoples."

"Why, No-Eyes? Why bother?"

Silence.

"I know God gives people a full length of rope. I know He has unbounded mercy and compassion, but thousands of people don't believe in the changes. They don't believe in the truths. They don't believe in the heritage gifts of the Great Spirit. They won't believe what I've written about you and they won't believe what I've said about myself. Why bother with them anyway? I still find it awfully hard to care at this late date. It's sort of after the fact to me."

"Would the Great Spirit leave one lost sheep behind?"

"That's relevant and explicit, but I'm not God. I don't possess His perfect qualities. I don't claim to be perfect. . . ."

"What so! *Nobody* here perfect. They not be here even."

"I know, but still. If people are continually turning their heads away and closing their ears and eyes to people like us, then I don't see why we have to bat our heads against the wall trying to convince anyone."

"That where Summer be all mix up."

I always thought everything was crystal clear to me.

"Summer and Bill not 'sposed to convince. That be force on peoples. See? Summer here to keep dropping seeds. Summer, Great Spirit want all peoples to know truth. It up to them to believe, make seed grow strong. Great Spirit need to have all peoples hear truths. It up to them to listen or close ears. Summer and Bill no convince peoples, no try even."

"I see, but I still think most people aren't open enough to believe. Some of the things I've written about you would seem like fantasy to them. How much credence does that give to the truths then?"

"Summer *no* see! Great Spirit fantasy? He even say He give gifts to peoples. He even say peoples do great stuff (miracles) too! What peoples think He mean? Great Spirit in spirit of all peoples. All peoples only look inside to see truth. They know, here, see then!"

"Don't be angry with me, No-Eyes, but I'm still having a hard time seeing my way through this. You've been saying we're only supposed to know the truth ourselves. . . ."

"Summer already know that."

"Let me finish. We're supposed to know the truth. Then, we're supposed to share it with those who also know it and. . . ."

"Not only peoples that also know it, Summer. Summer and Bill share with peoples who on right path but need more information even. See?"

"I was getting to that part. We're not supposed to try to convince anyone. We're supposed to set up The Mountain Brotherhood for seekers who need additional information. The Mountain Brotherhood is to give answers to requested information and questions. It's to occasionally give a comforting atmosphere to those kindred souls who request a physical meeting or discussion."

"That right."

"No-Eyes, Bill and I need some peace for awhile. We don't want people coming all the time."

"What so! No-Eyes no say Summer have peoples all time. Summer and Bill have special time for peoples coming."

"You mean like appointments?"

"NO! Think!"

"I know! We could set up an evening time for casual discussions. Maybe one every week or every other week! And whoever shows up will be able to discuss with us and the others."

"That sound better."

"I think that sounds better too. It'd be more like friends getting together for a quiet evening. It'll be like friends with the same beliefs gathering around and sharing." It sounded too good to me.

"Summer, what so some peoples want know how to make spirit fly? What Summer do 'bout that?"

"I don't know. I never thought of that. I suppose I'd have to look into them and decide individually. I don't really expect to run a school!"

Silence.

"Do I?"

Silence.

"No-Eyes, you're being rather uncooperative here."

Silence.

"Well, we're *not* running a school. The Mountain Brotherhood is for kindred spirits to get together in a loving and sharing atmosphere. It's only an information center. People can write and we'll answer back, but it's certainly not a school! And don't you tell me it is!"

"Nope. It no school."

Relief.

"Teaching scare Summer?"

"No, don't forget I ran my own dance school. Teaching doesn't scare me at all, it's just that I was sure that wasn't our purpose. It's more like providing the proper atmosphere for believing friends."

"That right—now."

"You're referring to before?"

"Yep. Before, Bill 'sposed to be teacher. He return to be leader of new spiritual physical community. Summer told of change. Now, it only for information. That better, huh."

"A lot better, but just as important."

"Not *just*! It *most* important even. Peoples' spirit most important than body even."

Silence.

"What Summer think heavy on?"

"No-Eyes, do you know where our center is going to be located?"

"Yep."

"Well where?"

"Here, in the mountains." She was teasing me.

"I knew that! What we want to know is where in the mountains."

"Friend tell that one."

"He said there were nine or ten possibilities, even as far away as Breckenridge."

"Summer no believe?"

"Of course I believe, but I'm not sure I want to go that far."

"Summer need more faith."

"I hardly think so. What do you think got us this far?"

Silence.

Waiting.

"Summer see. It all gonna work out."

"Then you're not going to answer my question about where the center will be?"

"Summer and Bill know when see it."

"That's a cop-out."

"*No* cop-out! Summer know it true."

"Yeah, I suppose. I just wanted to save a little footwork and time."

"Time enough."

"But we do feel the pressure from the other side."

"Yep. That keep Summer and Bill on toes."

"All the time? No-Eyes, I said we needed a rest."

"Summer and Bill gonna get that. Maybe little one."

"Tell me about the others." I changed the subject.

"What others?"

"*No-Eyes!*" She was purposely making me dance in circles.

"Summer no mood for game, huh. Okay. Many other new peoples all over now. They remember purpose too. They gonna start many communities for peoples to live in. They gonna get many lands. They gonna show peoples how to share lands for farming foods, raising animals. Many aware peoples already starting new life on these lands. They doctors and big job peoples [professionals] too. They work hard for all peoples of land community. They gonna be ready good when the time come. Summer look puzzled. What now?"

"I feel bad for the people who won't believe."

"Summer say Summer no care."

"I still feel bad for them."

"That peoples' choice, Summer. It not be Summer's fault."

"I realize that, but it doesn't make it any better. Whenever I'm downtown and I see all those tract houses piled so tightly together like lined-up matchboxes I always think, 'My God, what are these people going to do!' No-Eyes, what *are* they going to do?"

"That life peoples want, Summer. They want stuff. They love stuff. They got only stuff when time come."

"But is that fair?"

"Is stuff fair not to listen? Summer tell No-Eyes peoples won't believe. That fair? Peoples got Great Spirit's free will. They hear, they see, they choose! It up to all peoples—inside!"

"But they're going to be so shocked and confused. They're going to have nothing!"

"No! Summer no think that way. They be shock, yep! But they already been told. Think! They be shock 'cause they no believe other peoples. It peoples' choice they end up no stuff [safe places and storage supplies]. They have own stuff!"

"Isn't that being awfully hardnosed? Sure, they'll have their big houses and fancy cars and expensive things. But No-Eyes, they won't have gasoline, electricity or food!"

"That peoples' choice."

Silence.

"Summer think that mean? Cold?"

Silence.

"Summer no can hurt for other peoples. Summer have to control that stuff."

"I can't. I feel so many miseries of the hungry. I feel the horrors of what's to come for the unbelievers who won't listen."

"If Summer no can stop, Summer need to understand better even."

Silence.

"Summer need to see how Great Spirit do stuff. He feel bad too. He give truths to peoples. He give heritage gifts to better see proof of truths. He give peoples free will. He give peoples long, long rope. He give, give, give, and give more even. He give all peoples many chances. He give good guides like Bill's—like Summer's friend. He give teachers to peoples. He never stop giving. He show right path. He give many years' time to peoples. He gonna stop one day. One day He gonna come. He gonna make it stop. He gonna draw final line. He gonna put believers on one side and no believers on other. He gonna let peoples' vibrations shake and break Earth Mother. Believers be already ready— they be safe in groups. Others be confused—they no ready. They caught full of shame with pants down. They sorry they no listen. He sorry too—but it already too late, time over—it all settled then."

"Yeah," I sighed, "I see your point. If God finally draws the line then I guess I have to too."

"Yep. Time come now for Summer stop hurt for no believers. It already too late even. Summer only work with believers now. See?"

"Yes. That does make it easier."

136

"Summer feel time pressure. No more time for other peoples. Only time for new peoples get in place for return purpose—give believers time too. Too many years wasted even trying to convince other peoples. That all over. Okay?"

"Okay, No-Eyes. This takes a heavy burden off of us. I appreciate your explanation."

"Summer and Bill no make burden more heavy. It already be enough."

"At least we no longer have the farming community to start."

"Got bigger stuff now."

"I know, the spiritual aspect."

"Yep. Summer know who Bill's spirit be?"

"Yes, No-Eyes. Our friend took care of all that when he first came."

"That funny time. It scare Bill plenty!" She grinned wide.

"It sure took us off guard, I'll say that much."

"Summer and Bill comfortable with him now, huh."

"He's like Bill's buddy."

"That good, Summer. That way 'sposed to be."

"I know, No-Eyes. I know."

And so went our discussion of the new spirits who have returned for the express purpose of heralding in God's time on Earth. These spirits are returning at an accelerated rate. Most of them are entering adult bodies by merely exchanging one consenting spirit for one who wished to be in the physical for this great time of mankind. Many have lived here since birth, searched the path their restless spirits urged them on, recognized their mission and went about their all-important business.

No-Eyes eventually led our conversation back to our dear friend. By now you will have presumably come to the conclusion that Bill and I have access to an open line of communication with Bill's guide. Yes, I'll admit as much as that, but that's all. This has been an extremely private and special thing between us. Only one other living person, with the respectful exception of No-Eyes, knows about him and has had conversations with that guide, and that is our physical friend Robin.

I'm not going to discuss how he came, why he came, when he came or how we three converse with him. Some things exist on sacred ground and this is most definitely one of those things.

I would hope with all my heart that you, the reader, have had that special welling within your being that comes with the recognition of the truth. I am far from a perfect person. As No-Eyes so often reminded me, I wouldn't be here if I was. Time is indeed growing short. There isn't a day that goes by without me feeling the pressure of the future closing in one more day, marking off another sunset on our present way of living. I would wish you the sight to seek the truths, to recognize them, to hold them precious within your hearts. I would wish you the right direction on your life's trail to lead you to the safety of a surviving community. I would wish you restful nights, peace in your heart and God within your spirit.

Tomorrow— A Changed World

May your Spirit see the time signs,
And may your heart accept their truths.

The crisp autumn nights were rejuvenating to both body and spirit. Bill and I continued our nightly ritual of the late evening walks. This night was particularly beautiful. The bright silver disk high up in the sky showered us in its etheric light as we strolled on our mountain trail. We paused awhile in a clearing. The view of the mystical valley below us was bathed in the gossamer essence of God. All was still and silent except for the mesmerizing song of the meandering stream that cleverly caught the sparkles of wandering moonbeams and winked them up into our faces. The wind was also still, as if holding its mighty breath in anticipation of some great event. The moonlight filtered through the aspens and transformed the golden leaves into treasures of pieces-of-eight. Mother Nature, with her magical powers, was an accomplished adept. She was the high priestess, the sorceress, the white magician of all time. She gently touched the golden aspen leaves with her wand of moonlight and worked her alchemy upon them, turning them into shining doubloons. The high firmament was alive with vibrating movement. The stars danced and twinkled a multitude of colors. They were keeping time with the rhythm of nature's thundering heartsounds.

We sat on the mountain ridge and quietly absorbed the pure mountain vibrations undulating around us. They flowed through our beings and left the residual benefit of a great peacefulness. We had much to discuss this night, yet the massiveness of creation kept us in a silent awe. The innocence of nature was profound. Its purity was most inspiring. These sacred nights in our open cathedral give our two tired spirits the holy union they forever thirsted for. The opulence of our church was indeed immeasurable in terms of riches. We softly entered on a carpet of glistening emeralds. We sat on seats laced with gems of turquoise and pyrite. Our heady incense of sage and pine mixed delicately with woodsmoke. It drifted lightly through the clear air. The side aisles were crowded with bouquets of deep green kinnikinnick, heavy with berries of glossy rubies. The towering mountains reached their silvery spires high into the house of God. They sparkled with their moonlit gilt. Our cathedral roof was the masterful architectural handiwork of the Gods, for when we raised our heads, we were reduced to utter humility with the grand design of the universe. And in the center of all was our ever-burning orb of eternal light—the moon.

Our church had no man-made articles. It had no statues—we needed no reminders of where we were or Who resided there. Our church had no expensive stained glass windows—we had stars. Our church had no manufactured music—we had the symphony of the spheres. Our church had no Sunday-dressed people—we had all God's creatures to worship with. Our church had no collection basket—we gave ourselves totally over to the will of God. Our church had no sermon—we listened to the Spirit breathe. Our church had no representative priest, minister or rabbi—we opened our spirit's door and let the glorious Spirit of God step quietly in.

All of nature gave evidence of God's existence. If you took the time to open yourself to it you would be welcomed into the presence of God. No-Eyes forever could not understand why people felt it so necessary to worship the Great Spirit only one day a week and to have to do it in a special building. She was sad that people spent so much money on decorating their churches in richness, when that same money could be used to feed and clothe the poor. Most of all, she was grieved that the people of today confined the Spirit of God into a building.

We readily agreed with her. We, too, couldn't comprehend this. Bill and I were both raised in strict Catholic families, attended rigid Catholic schools, were married in the Catholic Church, yet, something profound was lacking. Puzzle pieces were missing. All things didn't cross-reference and we began searching for those lost pieces. We saw the extravagance of the church and wondered. We heard the dogmatic teachings and questioned. We saw major changes taking place and we saw the hand of man. We saw rigid rules—where was the boundless mercy of God? We saw our light and followed it.

Our children see a summer thunderstorm and they are aware of the power of God. They hear the weak chirps of hungry baby birds and they see how God provides for His children. They inspect a bird's nest and they know God gave certain instincts. They silently watch an elk step cautiously out of the forest line and they see the innocence of God's creatures. They observe the night heavens and they feel God's presence. They are not carted off between four walls once a week to recite memorized prayers. They create their own every day in our magnificent cathedral constructed by the loving hand of God.

Bill and I left our outside pew and began descending into the valley. Hand-in-hand we softly treaded through the reverent silence. We reached the swift-coursing stream and followed alongside. The mountains rose high above us on three sides. We were alone in the peaceful arms of nature. Neither of us desired to break the stillness, yet we had much to discuss.

I shattered the silence with my whisper. "No-Eyes had a lot to say today."

"I suppose she did. She always does."

"We talked about the end."

"Any specifics?"

"That's for another day. We talked about believers and the unbelievers."

"Pretty heavy subject, I'd say."

"Yeah."

We stopped to listen to a distant splashing. The beavers were going to work.

"Well, what'd she have to say?"

"She said I shouldn't worry about all those people downtown."

"I told you that."

"I know, but she put it in a different light."

"Oh?"

"She said that God's going to draw a final line so why shouldn't I."

"Clever way of putting it. She's right, you know. You can't keep feeling those bad things all the time."

"I only wish you felt them too, then you'd understand better."

He squeezed my shoulder. "Well, maybe now they won't be so strong. Maybe now you'll be able to shrug them off instead of letting them hurt you."

"I hope so, we've got enough going on without extra negative burdens."

"So, what else did she say?"

"She brought up the Brotherhood. We went around and around again. She was in a good mood and tried joking. I guess I wasn't in the mood. Anyway, she knew all about it and confirmed that it'd be an information center."

"Whew! I sure didn't want things to change again."

"No, don't worry. It's just going to be a center for sharing and answering mail."

"Sharing?"

"Yeah, she said we could have people stop by for informal evening discussions. You know, like two nights a month or whatever we decide."

"That sounds alright." He tickled my ribs. "Wouldn't it be nice having a real honest sharing with other believers?"

"Sure would. But No-Eyes also wanted to see my reaction when she asked me what I'd do if some of those people wanted to learn her lessons."

"Oh boy, that makes a difference, doesn't it. What'd you say to that?"

"I told her we weren't running a school."

"Good."

"But I did say it would depend on what I saw in the individual. I think it'd depend on circumstances and how each group interacted, don't you?"

"I'm not sure. I'm not sure we should get into that. For one thing, her lessons are real complicated, it'd take more time than one evening just to get through one lesson. No, I don't think it'd be a good idea. I think what'll happen is the group will meet on specified days of the month. We'll welcome whoever wants to join in that night, and we'll just sit around and talk about whatever they like. That sounds like friends sharing a casual evening."

"I think so too."

"You could always describe her techniques in a step-by-step instruction book."

"No, I don't want to do that. You can't put those things in books. Honey, remember how No-Eyes followed me whenever she had me go somewhere? I can't do that with people reading their lesson. They could get into real trouble. No, those lessons could never be on paper. They can only be experienced with a teacher who could watch what was going on."

"Yeah, I forgot about that. Some books show techniques, though."

"Not *hers*," I laughed.

He agreed. "She's some lady, isn't she."

"Yep!" I mimicked her.

We talked about the unbelievers as we walked back to the house. We came to the conclusion that it was indeed time for us to accept the choice they had made. From this night forward, we would expend our energies on helping those seekers who were led to us. We no longer were involved in searching out people. A portion of our burden was lifted off. And it felt wonderful.

My next meeting with the old woman was on Tuesday of the following week. While driving out to her place I felt a touchable reticence to continue. I sensed a grave and serious discussion coming on. The day was glorious and I felt like hell. As I pulled off the road and turned the engine off, I peered out the windshield and looked up the hill to her cabin. Smoke curled out of the old chimney. It was serene enough, yet I knew how surface peacefulness could be deceiving. Today was going to be spent in heaviness, my senses were forewarning me to be armed.

When I entered the warmth of the cabin, the old woman was meditating. I silently tip-toed to the couch and sat down. I carefully leaned back, closed my eyes and waited for her to return. The fire was burning softly and its hypnotising warmth lulled me into a restful sleep.

As the busy conscious mind rested, the spirit sped quickly away. I was far above the earth and it was beautiful. A slow rotating mass of blues and greens. A true masterpiece of the divine. I looked around. No-Eyes was behind me.

"Summer not take long as No-Eyes think."

"Your cabin was so cozy. It made me sleepy."

"It 'sposed to."

"Does everything of yours do what it's supposed to?"

"It better."

"I even did." I grinned.

"Yep, even Summer." She smiled back.

I looked down again. "It's beautiful, isn't it, No-Eyes. It looks so peaceful."

"Summer need closer look! It no full of peace."

We drifted down. We went through the upper atmospheric clouds. The view was so clear and visible. My mouth dropped open. I couldn't take my eyes from it as the great planet slumped on its side. It wobbled, then appeared to stabilize.

"Earth Mother in great pain. She rearranging herself."

I was fascinated. I had met the old woman in the fine ether of the future.

"We gonna go see." She went forward.

I followed, filled with wild curiosity. I followed her above the area of the United States. I barely recognized it. Before, it was hard enough to tell where the different states were. I was always used to looking at the line divisions on a map. Now, I definitely needed her keen eye and expert narration.

We surveyed the entire continent of North America. The familiar geographic shape was changing its format at a rapid rate. We watched the movements as though we were viewing it through a child's ever-changing kaleidoscope. Yet, this was no game. The earth was no toy. This was real. Everything had tilted down to the right. Alaska was now the tip of North America. Mexico wasn't south anymore, but rather west. New York was only partially visible.

On a closer inspection, we found that all of North America's east and west coasts were gone. Florida appeared to be ripped entirely off the continent. The major fault lines had cracked. The San Andreas ripped through the land like some giant tearing a thin piece of paper. The torn shred drifted out into the churning ocean.

The waters of the world literally swished back in one huge movement, paused and came surging back to seek a new level of balance. This great movement washed over hundreds of islands. Hawaii was gone completely. Borneo, Sumatra, Philippines, Japan, Cuba, United Kingdom—all vanished within a blink of an eye!

We closed in on the United States. It wasn't as wide anymore due to the lessening of coastal areas. The Mitten State, Michigan, was covered with angry rushing waters. Upper Michigan had been torn away with the force of Lake Superior's emergency exit. All the Great Lake waters were forging downward, following the Mississippi River. Massive land areas on either side of the Mississippi River were flooded out of view. A great trench was being dug by the powerful force of the rushing waters. The land area below Michigan was drowned. Water was everywhere. There was no land under an imaginary line from Houston to somewhere around Raleigh, North Carolina. Most of New York, Pennsylvania and Ohio were under water. *All* of Michigan and Indiana were. The United States was now divided completely. The eastern portion was an island.

"Water go back down later. Not always be island."

I was relieved to hear that. This was so incredible. When the time came for these changes, it would be a long time before the survivors were able to get a true and accurate picture of the extent of damage. I looked far to my left and saw that all of the coastal land west of the Sierra Nevadas was gone.

144

A large portion of the Appalachian Range split and spread out. The Great Divide appeared to be fairly untouched. Volcanoes spewed in much of the western section of the land.

"We gonna go closer."

"This is close enough." I didn't want to see the people.

"Summer remembers dream, huh."

I nodded.

"Summer need to see. We go now."

I reluctantly followed her beautiful spirit.

The view of the earth grew large as if we were watching it through a telescoping lens. We descended directly above Omaha, Nebraska.

I felt as if I was watching some horror movie conceived in the mind of evil. Horrible scenes were graphically played out in vivid detail. The city was in ruin. Evidently a strong tremor swept through the city. The tall buildings were left in their nakedness of iron skeletons. Concrete and glass lay scattered about in huge piles of rubble. People ran amok screaming in hysterics. Gore was everywhere. Crushed and mutilated bodies lay in agony over the dead. Fires burned like torches from the gas lines. Hot electrical wires lay sparking. It was total chaos.

We drifted out into the suburbs. The scenes here were less massive in destruction, but they were typical of the larger city. The low buildings were leveled and the ones still standing were being attacked by hordes of mindless people. They swarmed in every store that had any kind of food. They trampled each other, caring little for the injuries they were inflicting upon the humans underneath their feet. I couldn't believe that civilized mankind could so quickly be reduced to such animal instincts of survival. They were down to the basest of actions. They were shooting one another. They were in throngs; some just roaming about, some storming private homes in an effort to get whatever they could find. The owners were shooting into the crowds. They were desperately trying to defend their domain. Animals ran wild. The zoo had been affected by the quake and cages were twisted, loosening wires and gates. The wild creatures were confused with their sudden freedom. Lions and cougars mauled screaming people. Elephants stampeded in a herd, trying to remain together. Reptiles roamed the streets. I felt sick. I had the presence of mind to think of the cabin.

My body was warm. The small room was silent. I opened my eyes and let them feast on the calm atmosphere. Yet, yet my ears were still vibrating from the roar and the screams of the future.

No-Eyes opened her eyes and stared straight ahead. She gently began to rock. Creak—thud. Creak—thud.

145

I softly spoke. "Why'd you have to do that?"

"It needed."

"I didn't need that. I had a pretty good idea how horrible it's going to be."

"Idea not same as knowing, feeling."

"You can say that again."

Creak—thud. Creak—thud.

Silence

Creak—thud. Creak—thud.

"No-Eyes, why can't America be like Switzerland? Do you know that they are prepared for such things?"

"Yep. No-Eyes see that just now."

"It's too bad we aren't."

"Yep. It too bad."

I laughed slightly. "No-Eyes, about a year ago a Colorado Springs paper printed an emergency plan in case of a national disaster. It was such an obvious farce! I couldn't believe it was for real. I couldn't believe the government was serious and that people believed it. No-Eyes, this plan had people taking a supply of food in their cars and driving to relief centers or up into the mountains. Could you just see such an alleged orderly exit in the face of a major disaster? It was utterly ridiculous!"

"That sad."

I stopped raving. "Yes, it is. It's very sad."

"What Summer feel?"

"You've brought back all my old empathy again. You've made my urgent pressure of time return. I just got rid of those and you've brought them all back."

"No need."

"How can I *help* it! Am I *not* supposed to feel their agonies? Am I *not* supposed to feel more pressure to get going to spread the word?"

"Summer, today no different than yesterday even. No need to feel different. Stuff all same both days."

I thought a minute about what she had said.

"I realize that, but the memory of what's coming haunts me. It'll intrude on my days. . . . "

"*No!* That only if Summer let that! Summer need to put all stuff in right place! What stuff we see all peoples doing, that all people's fault. Great Spirit let peoples' vibrations go. He not let spirits control stuff no more times. He tell spirits stop protecting Earth Mother. He say it time to let go! It time for peoples to see stuff they make with thoughts, stuff peoples make with way peoples live even! Summer, *peoples* make all that stuff happen. It be peoples own *effect!*"

"You're right. They'll bring that on all by themselves."

"Yep! That big part of cleaning Great Spirit gonna do. That His beginning."

"I keep forgetting that. I keep forgetting that God will be allowing the masses to punish themselves."

"That right! Summer no forget that! That important stuff. That reason for change even."

"I've got a lot to do."

"Plenty time yet even."

"How much time is plenty?"

She stopped rocking. She was silent.

"*No-Eyes!*"

The meter started up again. "Got 'bout sixteen years even—maybe."

"Maybe?"

"Stuff gonna come before that even."

"War?"

"Yep."

Oh great! As if I didn't have enough to worry about. "*What* war?"

"Big one over world."

"World War *Three*?" I nearly leaped off the couch.

"*Sit down!*" she shouted.

I didn't. I paced the floor. "I can't sit down. Tell me what you're talking about!"

She rocked obstinately—in silence.

I paced around with my anxiety attack.

She finally spoke in an even and calm manner. "Summer calm down before No-Eyes say stuff."

I quickly sat back on the couch. I waited nearly ten minutes before she again spoke.

"Summer more calm now. No-Eyes finish stuff now before No-Eyes got interrupted so bad."

"I'm sorry, but you really threw me a curve. You sprung that on me out of the blue."

"Summer 'sposed to be used to unexpected stuff."

"You know damned well I am."

"That look like it. Summer no swear."

"If that's all I ever do in life then I'm not worried."

"That okay. Summer do alright in life."

"Now that we have that cleared up, I'd like to hear about this war. When is this coming?"

"What war?"

Silence.

I'd had enough of our ridiculous merry-go-round conversations. I was sick of verbally chasing my tail. I fumed in angered silence.

She rocked in our silence. She was giving me time to think.

And I did. I thought of all the nonsensical discussions we'd had and how they always served to clarify the subject. She led me in verbal circles until my own realizations led us out. I thought about what an expert teaching mind she possessed. She always made the student find the answers. The verbal mazes were for the benefit of giving the learner proper experience in thinking things out for themselves. Then my thoughts drifted into the future discussions Bill and I would have with those stranger/friends who would come to share with us. I saw myself leading the circle dance with them. I was ashamed for blowing up at my old patient teacher. "I'm sorry."

"What so! No-Eyes know that. No-Eyes wait for Summer to know that."

She was incredible. God, she was understanding! "I'll listen now."

"Summer, it *your* turn for answer. No-Eyes say 'what war?'"

"Oh yeah." I needed more thinking time. I thought aloud. "Well, if you're asking me that, then I assume the war won't actually escalate into a full-fledged World War. A war will begin somehow, and it will also be stopped somehow. And from other insinuations you've made, I gather there will be *some* adverse affects in our country. If this is coming before the changes, then it'll come within the next fifteen years and . . . ."

"*Look!*" she ordered, pointing to the floor.

I stared at the thin, braided rug. I stared until my concentration was so centered I saw nothing but a fuzziness closing in. A smokey wavering covered my vision. I saw a year. I blinked and looked at my waiting teacher. "That's a lot sooner than I expected it would be."

"Yep. It come from Africa."

"But the Watchers will stop it, won't they?"

"Yep. Soon after stuff start, they gonna take control."

"I guess it wouldn't do to have the world destroyed before God lets the people do that themselves."

"Nope."

"No-Eyes, we really don't have much time at all then, do we?"

"Summer gonna be fine."

"I believe that because I have faith in what you see."

"Summer have faith in what *Summer* see!"

Silence.

"No-Eyes, I'm tired. Will you tell me what the effects of this will be?"

"Humph! Summer no gonna get lazy!" Then she softened. "Summer no lazy. Summer just tired. No-Eyes tell."

"Thanks."

"Big bombs gonna go across sky. One, maybe two more even come here. It enough to stop power. It upset Earth Mother. She gonna shake—upset gas under earth. They gonna stop that. No more bombs come then. See?"

She was telling me that missiles would be exchanged, but only a few. The missiles would target areas of major power, communication and arsenal areas. Perhaps the first missiles would explode above ground and initially inhibit power. She referred to the Earth Watchers and that they would use their highly advanced technology to stop the exchanges. These Earth Watchers are intelligent beings who are concerned about the welfare of the earth, in respect to possible adverse chain reactions out into the universe. We had several lengthy discussions regarding this subject. It was quite involved, yet enlightening to know that mankind was not going to be allowed to annihilate himself or his beautiful world. She inferred that they would prevent such an unfortunate occurrence by using a force field that was as yet incomprehensible to us. This unknown force field would disintegrate the missiles on contact. There were many concepts that I found terribly complex for my conditioned mind. Some concepts dealt with trying to grasp the understanding of more dimensions. Other concepts involved a complete re-thinking of physics theories. I had studied chemistry and physics, yet some of her concepts were direct opposites and she proved them. Our world has a long way to travel. Our scientists need more open minds if they are ever going to advance us further. But that is another subject all together, isn't it.

"I'm glad a real war won't become a reality."

"Stuff still gonna change, Summer."

"Yeah. If mechanical instruments will be affected, I'm sure we'll have to make some radical changes for awhile. If the arsenals are blown, that will be physically devastating to certain geographical areas. I can also see the consequences of pipelines of natural gas exploding too. You haven't painted a very pretty picture, but at least it won't annihilate us like a full-scale war would've."

"No-Eyes no paint picture. It already there even."

"I know. That was just a figure of speech."

"Summer think Summer smart. Say stuff No-Eyes no know."

"Now who's being smart."

"See? Summer find some fun."

"I guess since I have no way of changing anything, I have to accept the inevitable."

"Yep. Summer have to accept."

We discussed the coming changes on the earth.

"Too bad peoples no see signs."

"What are you talking about, No-Eyes?"

"Sign stuff. Many signs 'bout changes right by peoples' noses even! They blind! They no see!"

"You mean the earth signs."

"Yep. What else?"

"I know what you mean. You know, several years ago Bill and I had a big wall map of the world. Everytime we read or heard about an earthquake or volcano or any other abnormal occurrence, we marked the spot with a black circle. Before long that map was so marked up we gave up. We could see a definite escalation of events though. I guess that was when our friend came to us."

"That when, alright."

"But even today, with all the abnormal weather systems, people still don't make the connection. They just sit back and click their tongues and talk about how strange things are. They'll never see the writing on the wall, even when it's spelled out."

"Yep. They blind alright."

"And it's not only the weather that's pointing the way. Disasters are occurring more often too; train wrecks, plane crashes, freak accidents where hundreds of people are killed. Look at the unrest around the world. *Still* people don't put the pieces together."

"Nope. Great Spirit's helpers been told to stop. They no more stop that stuff. Great Spirit gonna let stuff go now."

"I know. He told us that. More and more disasters will be happening more frequently. So many signs—so many."

"Yep." Creak—thud. Creak—thud.

My Heart is on the Ground

*May I ever treasure the memory
of No-Eyes,
And may I never stop hearing
her glorious Spirit Song.*

It was winter. And all the earth was purified. The sleeping aspens were lovingly covered in a handmade quilt, a quilt Mother Nature carefully stitched with glistening threads of white sparkle. The silent world of winter glittered in the light of the early morning sun. The thick blanket warmly insulated the tiny creatures from the frigid breath of the North wind.

The white icing over the twisting stream was elaborately decorated with the Earth Mother's own flamboyant signature. Dainty swirls and feathery streaks gave evidence to her natural flair for beauty. Beneath the layered frosting, the old waters bubbled and rushed over and between the granite rocks, surging downstream to break away and burst forth in a torrent of cascading freedom.

The sun's morning rays broke over the far mountain peak. They flooded the valley in a mystical light, a light that touched the threads of the great quilt and made it jump to life with shimmering orange reflections. The alpenglow on a winter morn is a flight into fantasy. My winter world was a magnificent masterpiece of God. It took my breath away. The total isolation of one person amid such abundance of purity and silence was nothing less than a miracle.

A blue shadow passed over me. I looked up into the blinding clear azure sky and observed the resident peregrine falcon gliding silently through his magic kingdom. I desperately desired to join him this fine morning of crystal clarity. I wanted to fly beside him; spread my wings wide, feel the fresh winter air in my nostrils, let my heart leap and sink in time with the soar and dive, yet I couldn't remain this day. I had business with the old woman and, I suppose, I was already long overdue. I gave the high flyer a last envious glance and slowly trudged up the hill.

Grey smoke thickly snaked up from the old chimney. I loved the little cabin. It had become my home away from home. It was crudely constructed, yet, to me, it was a golden palace. Its furnishings were worn and meager, yet they were richly appointed in my eyes. I saw a place where I could be warmly welcomed, a place filled with love and friendship, a place brightly lit by the light of a blazing fire.

"No-Eyes think Summer no come today."

I chuckled. "You expect me to believe that?"

"Summer much late! What No-Eyes think?"

"You knew I'd be here."

"Summer need no sleep so late."

"I was up bright and early."

She turned her head to the frosted window. "What so! Then Summer no be so long down in valley!"

"See! I knew you knew."

She grinned. "Earth Mother happy today, huh."

"She sure is."

"Summer want fly today?"

"No. I'd just like to sit around the fire again."

"Winter gonna make Summer fat!"

"Never." I sat on the floor by the fireplace. I wrapped my arms about my knees and rested my chin on them.

No-Eyes sat on the floor next to me. She was silent.

We often sat together for a long while without either of us breaking the warm silence. It was our special way of sharing each other's being, our presence. That silence relayed more words of endearment than the most eloquent spoken words could have. The fire snapped and crackled. It flashed its flickering orange reflections over our pensive faces. We were content.

As the length of our silence increased, I picked up an irritating feeling in the room. It bothered me. I sharpened my senses. I felt no intruding presence within the confines of the cabin, yet something was very wrong. And it was coming from the quiet old woman. I inched closer and put my hand over her frail fingers. "What's wrong, No-Eyes?" I asked softly.

She shrugged the boney shoulders. "What so? Why Summer

think something wrong?"

"I think something's wrong because you've been a good teacher. I sense it, that's why."

She looked up at me. "Summer think she so smart, huh?"

"I think you've taught me well."

"Too good, maybe."

"Then tell me what's wrong."

"Summer not 'sposed to get in No-Eyes' head!"

"We're too close. It can't be helped anymore. Now tell me what's bothering you."

"No-Eyes be okay."

"You're not getting off so easy. I'm not moving until you tell me."

She heaved a great heavy sigh. Silence.

"I'm waiting."

"Summer stubborn."

"No more than you. Who taught me to be persistent? Who was my thorough teacher?"

Silence.

"Please?"

"No-Eyes be sad."

I had seen her sad only once before and that was when she instilled a memory of the People into my mind. It was an extremely exhaustive and emotional experience for both of us. I couldn't imagine what had suddenly caused her present state of such a deep melancholy. I didn't think she was going to tell me either. I stopped all conscious thoughts. I reached far back into the old one's mind. A great hand pulled hard on my heartstrings. My throat was constricted. "*No!* I won't *let* you go!"

She patted my hand. "Summer no can help."

"Of course I can! You can come to live with *us*! We'll take care of you *always*!"

She got up and sat in her chair. She was silent.

I moved over next to her and put my hands on her lap. I held onto the thin brown hands. "You *can't* go away. Where are you going?"

She put one hand on my head. "Summer, No-Eyes tell 'bout Chippewa friends here in mountains. We all gonna go back home soon. No-Eyes all done here."

I was upset. I was near hysterics. "But you can let *them* go! I mean, *you* don't have to go *too*! *This* is your home!"

"Summer," she whispered lovingly, "this only be schoolroom. No-Eyes need go home for stuff. No-Eyes need go pretty soon even."

"I don't understand. *Why* do you have to go home? You've been

153

here for years! Please, No-Eyes, *please* don't leave!" I began crying.

She gently pushed my head down on her lap. She stroked my hair as I cried. "Summer, No-Eyes be done with stuff. No-Eyes finish here. No-Eyes *all* done."

Those few simple words spoken so tenderly thundered through my world with the force of a thousand buffalo. I couldn't believe what I was hearing. I didn't want to believe it. I was devastated to think I'd lose my beloved old friend. She was leaving me. I cried great sobs as I crushed her dress in my clutching fingers. I held her waist, I held on as tight as I could. It wouldn't be tight enough, nothing could be. I knew what she was saying. *God!* why did I have to understand!

She continued to stroke my hair. I felt a drop of wetness fall on my forehead.

"It gonna be okay, Summer. Old teachers gotta go. New teachers gotta come. That way 'sposed to be. No-Eyes gonna be on way. Summer gonna be on way. That way 'sposed to be." No-Eyes began to gently rock with my head on her lap.

I knew she was crying. I was crying. We remained that way, silently grasping for each other's essence while we still could. The fire crackled. And outside, the winter wind whipped the corners of the blanket up around the lone cabin that held two women within its warm walls; one just finding her home, the other just going home— going home to die.

Afterword

I was heartbroken for days after that emotional winter day with No-Eyes. The fact that she was going home was sad enough, but the knowledge that she was going home to die devastated me. Bill tried his hardest to help me overcome my deep grief and sense of impending loss. His great compassion and sympathy were valiant attempts, yet this was something I had to hurdle myself.

As the weeks went by and the winds of winter blustered about the old cabin, I went to see No-Eyes as often as I could. Amazingly enough, there were actually times we were able to forget about the terrible day when she would no longer be there. My lessons were over. We spent long hours talking of the things I had learned; things of the future, how I should handle her lessons. We discussed the plight of the seekers, the confusing path of those seekers, how to help, how to show compassion and understanding—love and light.

Our days were beautiful. Our unique bond was a nearly visible thing. We visited all winter long. She told me it would be awhile before her friends were leaving. We still had much time.

Winter gave way to spring. The fresh mountain air was heavy with a new sweet scent. I was anxious to get to her cabin. I never stopped along the way anymore. I was fearful of cutting short our remaining time. I pulled the truck up and while climbing her hill I noticed her front door was open. I figured she was letting the fresh air in. I could hear her moving about inside. She must have dropped something, for I heard glass shatter.

I ran up the steps to see if I could help her. I stopped short when I reached the opened door. The cabin was empty!

My heart sunk into my stomach. I felt sick. I stepped in just as a raccoon darted quickly past my feet. It had been rummaging about in the bare kitchen. I was numb. I hypnotically moved through the living room. She had given all her furniture away, just like she said she would. I felt sick.

I entered the tiny kitchen. My footfalls echoed their loneliness. I opened the cupboards. Empty jars, jugs, boxes and bottles gaped back at me. She returned their contents to the Earth Mother, just like she said she would. I ran my hand over the glass of the window. The sky was clear, just like it was the day we flew with the falcon. I rested my head against the window and I cried like a baby.

A beam of sunlight reached in and blinded me. I wiped my red eyes and walked back to the door. I stood in the doorway and surveyed the room for the last time. I didn't see bare walls. I saw firelight flickering over them. I didn't see a cold stone fireplace. I saw a crackling blazing fire. I didn't see a bare room. I saw a rocker that gently went creak and thud. I didn't see the darkness inside. I saw a cabin that was once filled with love, a cabin that was once brightly illuminated by the visionary wisdom of a gentle old woman.

It was a precious part of my past, and gently, very gently I closed the door.